The State of Boone

THE STATE OF BOONE

The tales we tell, the ones we've been told & the stories
we should never forget

Kassie Ritman

Knocking River Press

Indianapolis

Contents

Introduction

In 2015 I spent lots of time collecting photos while writing *Boone County* for Arcadia Publishing. All my hours yielded a "history in hand" book with over 200 photos and captions. While digging for old images and facts, some of the quirky tales and events I bumped into just begged for more words and attention.

The stories you'll find on these pages required more than a brief caption to be told. Researching for *The State of Boone* shed light on many rumors we've all grown accustomed to "accepting." In more than one case, the closest thing to the truth laid buried within the variations of retelling passed from one generation to the next. Here, I get to share the important people, places, and things teetering on the brink of being forgotten.

The State of Boone, is meant as a starting point for the reader; a road map to jump-start memories and spark conversation. Readers are invited to began an adventure within the pages; triggering recollections of having heard these stories, while also discovering some surprising new ones. Much of Boone County history is intertwined within its own current citizenry. Over and over I was shocked by the things I never knew; I hope you will have the same experience of discovery.

And yes, I know a few eyebrows will rise up in defiance. Some of these tales are old, longstanding legends. Many will find carved-in-stone beliefs challenged. In the past, just as in our modern lives, there existed the cocktail-party version of an event often colliding head-on with court records, newspaper reports, and accounts given by firsthand observers. The pages I've written come from composites cobbled together by chasing down as many versions of a story as possible. Where there is an incongruity of the facts, I've tried my best to discern the truth.

If you find yourself disagreeing, I encourage you to use the book's margins and blank spots to add your own two-cents. I love co-authors, and have shared these tales fully hoping that they will be enjoyed and "corrected" by many generations of Boone-connected families. Your own version certainly deserves to be recorded along with the ones printed here.

I'm a firm believer that history holds a shelf life of around 100 years. After that, if an event has not been preserved in some fashion, it's destined to be lost forever into the tangle of time. Don't let your own family stories or connections to these Boone County treasures slip through the cracks.

Work on making this "book of lore" your own. Customize it any way you'd like. Freely add some tucked-in pages, a few hand written notes next to names, or a full-on explanation of why the version presented here is just flat-out wrong. Point of view is what family history is all about, and in the end, The State of Boone is a part of our families–no matter how thin our connection to this wonderful place.

———————

Here's to all the Boonites, near and far–May these stories strike you with gratitude, knowing they weren't allowed to fade away!

———————

Want more stories, guidance and tips on how to start writing your own family history?
Go to www.WritingWithMom.com
or follow me on
Facebook at Author Kassie Ritman

Acknowledgements

Sincerest thanks to all who helped with the making of this book. Some shared stories, or pointed me toward hidden sources or people who might know more. Some helped to decode old writing or carvings. Others were kind enough to let me go traipsing across their lawn to view a tucked-away grave site. Many shared the story of their historic home or farm. I was encouraged to start by old friends, and blessed with countless new friendships along the way. One thing I know for certain–Boone County is a friendly, off-beat and lovely-hearted place to be from. If you helped out, and I forgot to thank you, please accept my apologies.

With greatest gratitude and heart-felt thanks to:

Robin and Glen Rabanus, Susan Luse, Jamey Hickson, Eric Spall, Jane Hammock, Phyllis Meyers, Dick Birge, Todd Snyder, Aaron Ballard, Kenny (Mooch) Lowe, The Adair family, Penny Brogan, John Glendenning, Michael Vetman, Lisa Cangany, The Everett Family, Rod and Dorothy Sutphin, Enid Cokinos, Marjie Gates Giffin, Judy Miller, Becky Laurenzana, Cindy Murphy, the Lovely Ladies of the Boone County Recorder's and Clerk's offices...and everyone who gave me directions when I got lost (which happened often!).

Cover photo of the Boone County Courthouse (home of the World's Largest Limestone Monoliths) from the Ralph W Stark Heritage Room Image Collection of the Lebanon Public Library

------

All other images from the private collection of the author except where otherwise noted

The Forgotten Graveyard

$$\sim\!\!\infty\!\!\sim$$

"Ownership in Cedar Hill was never vested in an individual or an organization. No maps or records have been found, but to say that there were some twelve hundred burials made in it, in the four decades from 1832, would be a conservative estimate." (Ralph W Stark)

On a humid May night in 1979, I joined a group of girls at the base of Lebanon's Water Tower. Meeting up just east of downtown on Park Street, we had plans for a midnight escapade. Ramped-up on nervous giggles and a single shared six pack of Little Kings, we'd gathered to watch the guys of our graduating class defy death. The girls were present as ground-support to the boys we awaited to climb the dew-coated ladder to the tower's top.

A dozen girls were milling around, conspiring and giggling. This evening was to mark the crowning event of our class's long list of "Senior Pranks." The gals had prepped for the mission bringing flashlights, wide brushes, and any half-used bucket of paint we could grab from our basements and barns. While waiting for the boys to arrive, we fine-tuned the plan. Looking far up into the night sky, we guesstimated our total supplies on hand and laughed some more.

Our goal was to emblazon a "79" across the pale blue face of the tank; immortalizing our graduating class.

As the courthouse clock stood hands-up at twelve, we agreed on the optimal spot. The big '79 would be most visible right below Lebanon's slogan "the Friendly City." We hoped the boys would be willing to climb that high.

To reach the bottom rung of the tower's ladder required a boost from the bed of a pickup truck. From there, the ascent was probably much longer than it looked from the ground. We had no inkling how far the face of that tank stood overhead. Our collected paint was unmatched in color and type–some was oil based, some whitewash, some matched mom's latest dining room walls. None of that mattered though, the real focus was to get the numbers painted on the face before daybreak; more importantly, before the cops showed up to chase us away.

By 12:30 there wasn't a single boy in sight. With our beer gone and no girls willing to climb, excitement faded. We soon disbanded; heading home, all of us hoping to slip-in unnoticed after curfew.

The co-conspiring boys offered no excuse for failing to come out that night. No matter; even without completion our mission had been fun enough. Most of the entertainment value was in the scheming and anticipation.

The Class of '79 never rescheduled the grand prank. Instead, we forgot about it and left the sun-bleached face of the water tower unmarred. Graduation day came. We went our separate ways. Facing forward, no one bothered to look back on what was left undone.

Oh, had I known then, what I know now!

I'm sure none of the other girls knew either; perhaps some never will. I do wonder if someone tipped off the boys. Was that why they blew us off? Did they know all along and never mentioned it–fearing we'd call them wussies?

Laughing under the water tower that night we didn't have a clue what our fashionable heels were poking into. No one noticed the terribly uneven turf. We were too busy having fun, waiting for manpower, the stroke of midnight; focused on defacing the tank. All of us were fully oblivious to the hundreds of unmarked graves beneath us.

Seriously!?

Who knew there used to be a graveyard there? Who knew it was still there?

In 1832 a team of surveyors was tasked with laying out the town of Lebanon as the center of trade and governing for citizens of Boone County, Indiana. The hired group was experienced and knew all of the amenities a town-from-scratch required.

A plot of land bordering what was to become Park Street was set aside for public use as a cemetery. The planners and surveyors rightly predicted that within a few years, there would be many homes and churches established within the city limits of the new county seat. Individual churches wouldn't have room to establish on-site graveyards like their neighbors in the countryside. Town folk would have little space to bury their departed loved ones in back yard graves as was the custom of many farm families.

The small 1.15 acre lawn was casually labeled "cemetery." It was under the ownership of all, and the responsibility of none. Any spot adorned with flowers or neatly clipped grass stood out from the others. Lawn care only happened when performed by the deceased's family, or by gardeners hired privately to care for a specific section or grave.

As with most habits of humans, when time passes, so does memory. When memories fade, so do connections and an intimate sense of obligation. Consequently, after a generation or two, the majority of pioneer graves in the cemetery lay forgotten in a woeful state of neglect.

In a letter, Abner Longley (who bought and built on the first lot sold in the new city of Lebanon) disclosed the identity of the graveyard's first burial. Longley penned this remembrance after he moved out of Boone County in his later years. He wrote that an early neighbor of his "died in 1832 from delirium tremens or fits brought on by hard drink. Mr Benjamin Dunn was the first occupant in the common burying place of your dead."

A mere 40 years after opening, the city's public cemetery was overflowing with interments and danger. Tangled messes of brush, rodents, and dumped garbage meant the place had become an embarrassing eyesore. Already the yard was so full that a single new grave could not be opened without disturbing another. The weedy surface was riddled with ankle-breaking animal burrows and sinkholes. The uneven ground heaved and collapsed with the seasonal freeze and thaw cycle sending markers askew. Many stones were eroded by the elements or toppled by vandals. Record keeping was both informal and erratic at best. The humblest graves, if marked at all, used upright wood planks or crossed boards. Even native hardwoods were no match for harsh Indiana weather and Boone County's damp soil.

Making matters worse, the lack of burial vaults (still not mandated by law, but a requirement by rule in most cemeteries today) attracted tunneling vermin. Hungry animals eagerly chewed through coffins, destroying the tops or sides and making the containers quick to collapse. The unwelcome critters and their constant digging to meet up with gruesome new food sources added to the trip hazards on the surface above.

Years later, as contamination and ground leaching is better understood, one could speculate the soil was also loaded with toxins. Many Civil War Soldiers were shipped directly home from the battlefield for burial at the old cemetery. Their bodies were embalmed with a cocktail of dangerous chemicals including arsenic, lead, methyl, turpentine and formaldehyde.

Just as all was looking grim in the old graveyard, a set of coincidences was set into motion. Wealthy Lebanon businessman, Samuel Rodefer, saw a need and filled it. Purchasing a little over nine acres at the edge of town bordered by Prairie

Creek, he opened a new graveyard. Established in March of 1872, Rodefer Cemetery was an immediate success. The first burial was made within days of opening. A five year old, Fannie Earheart, was entered on the new cemetery's ledger as grave number one.

Handwritten records from Rodefer's show that soon after the first grave was dug, a rash of reburials occurred. Folks of means, and those able to borrow enough, began moving the final resting place of loved ones away from the horrific conditions at the old city cemetery to the verdant acres at Rodefer's.

Some report that as many as 2000 people were laid to rest at the old public cemetery. Others estimate that at least 500 were moved. Those removed were lifted out of their original burials to be re-interred during the first few years after Sam Rodefer opened his tidy new cemetery.

Today, walking through the oldest section of Oak Hill (the former acreage of Rodefer's) you'll notice several graves of folks who died *before* the graveyard's opening in 1872. These represent the many who were exhumed from the old public cemetery. In fact, the new place was so popular, some burials were even moved from private family graveyards in the country. Rodefer's was considered quite fashionable. Still others were moved to Rodefer Cemetery in name and spirit only; their remains being too long decayed, or just plain lost.

About 35 years after most burials ceased at the old cemetery, a cleanup and restoration project was initiated by a local women's group. Often attributed to the "Dames of the '60s," the group took their name from the historical decade when the Civil War was fought. After extensive work to clear brush and upright or repair damaged grave markers, the Dames also gave the old cemetery a name. Nearly 80 years had passed since Benjamin Dunn had drunk himself to death and taken up eternal residency in the nameless lawn. Finally, in 1907 the graveyard was officially proclaimed "Cedar Hill" and a fancy sign was placed on the revitalized grounds.

Unfortunately, the Dames' cleanup efforts were not

maintained. The demands of upkeep were constant and costly. By 1954 when the local James Hill Chapter of the Daughters of the American Revolution (DAR) stepped in, conditions were even worse at Cedar Hill. The place was both a shameful dumping ground and a threat to public health.

With documentation in hand proving their namesake's burial at Cedar Hill, the DAR ladies asked officials of the county seat for possession of the mess. Promised an extensive rehabilitation of the property, the city quickly agreed. Using grants and donations, the DAR undertook the arduous restoration work. Wading into the project, the women probably had no idea what they were up against. After decades of neglect, there was little to salvage on the raised knoll of weeds and garbage known as Cedar Hill.

No maps of burials we ever kept for the graveyard. There had never been formal record keeping at all; only scattered mentions within obituary notices, family bibles and private letters. Remaining headstones were faded, broken, knocked over and mostly illegible. Many had been displaced by invasive trees, storms or vandals. Several were lying in large piles at the corners of the property.

A difficult decision was made to remove all the grave markers. They were gathered and taken to a landfill property at the edge of town. Public notifications were posted inviting interested parties to freely claim the family stones which stood waiting in neat rows at the edge of the city dump. After a few months passed, the unclaimed markers were disposed of.

The entire yard was replanted with grass and a commemorative stone was placed on the property for Revolutionary War Soldier, James Hill. Originally from Virginia, Hill lived to see his 109th birthday at Lebanon. A flag pole was added, and a second stone monument was erected on the property with the following inscription:

Cedar Hill Cemetery
Founded 1832 Abandoned 1872
Markers Removed In 1954

Over 500 Citizens
Of Early Lebanon
Including 32 War
Veterans Sleep Here
Remember Us–For We Too
Once Lived And Served
This Community

After making these improvements and taming the overgrown brambles and piles of garbage openly dumped over the graves for many years, the DAR gifted Cedar Hill back to the City of Lebanon for community use, again renaming it; this time as James Hill Park. The town now uses the lawn as a home to the municipal water tower.

Feeling bitter or angry toward those 1954 DAR members for their treatment of Boone County's first public graveyard is easy. However, the real ire is better aimed at the original surveyors who portioned off the land without assigning ownership to any entity, group or office.

On one hand, there was no owner, thus no fee for burial. Clearly anyone who used the property could see what they were getting as an eternal resting place for loved ones. On the other, no one was keeping records or making rules or doing maintenance on the property. So it seems that everyone was to blame for the cemetery's demise– as much as no one was to blame for its ruin.

Those 1776
Headstones

If there must be trouble, let it be in my day, that my child may have peace." (Thomas Paine)

An amazing act of historical foresight and preservation began in 1896. That year, the membership of our local DAR chapter began seeking out and documenting the final resting spots of all Revolutionary War soldiers within Boone County's borders. Working diligently over the ninety years from 1896 until 1987, they were able to document burials of twenty men who had fought and served.

Heroes of our nation's Independence were found scattered across Boone in cemeteries both large and small. Money was raised and each confirmed grave was honored with a large, specially designed marker. Some were in church-yards, several were found in public cemeteries and a handful laid resting on family land. An unfortunate group of three are in graves no longer marked; their precise whereabouts unremembered. Though they aren't all physically accounted for, we still count them as ours somewhere under the rich soil of Boone County.

The "1776ers" are also honored as a group with a monument

placed by the DAR in 1935 at the southwest corner of courthouse square. The brass plate mounted on a granite boulder commemorates the service of these brave men to our fledgling country. Though in need of updating, the marker also reminds us of the lives they lived among the earliest pioneers of our newly settled bit of wilderness.

In reviewing the following list, you may recognize many Patriot's surnames. Most have direct descendants still living in Boone County today.

The 1776ers can be easily spotted by the large "1776" chiseled into the crown of the stone. Their names were recorded onto the special markers as spelled upon enlistment (sometimes conflicting with later or current spellings). Here are the 20, along with the names of the cemetery/site where they are located or thought to be.

If history has ever seemed remote to you, I urge you to make a visit to one of these graves in an accessible public graveyard. Take a moment to absorb the magnitude of what the man below your feet was part of. I guarantee your opinion of historical things, and your heart toward history in general, will be changed forever.

The Boone 1776ers In Alphabetical Order

- *John Aldridge* – Thought to be at a lost grave site on the outskirts of old Thorntown town limits, though not confirmed
- *Arthur Andrews* – Hopewell – North of Lebanon on Highway 47
- *Francis Brown* – Pleasant View – East of Dover
- *Samuel Dooley* – Mts Run – About 7 miles east of Lebanon
- *Jacob Foreman* – Thought to be in an obliterated cemetery under a road built in front of the old Royalton Methodist Church–unconfirmed
- *John Ferguson* – Cox – Thorntown / Northwest of Dover

- *William Gipson* – Gipson Cemetery -Private farm near Thorntown near Highways 52 and 47 (more than 1000 attended the dedication of his marker in 1898)
- *George W Grimes* – Cox – Thorntown/ Northwest of Dover
- *James Hill* – Cedar Hill Cemetery/ James Hill Park – Lebanon
- *Henry Johns Sr.* – Johns Cemetery – Union Township
- *John Kersey* – Beck's – Northwest of Lebanon on Highway 52
- *John Leap* – Mt Tabor Baptist – near Fayette (Leap died at age 112!)
- *John McManus* – May be unmarked at Mt Tabor Baptist near Fayette, or, more probably in the defunct Methodist cemetery partially covered by a road expansion project at Royalton, though not confirmed
- *William Pauley* – Precinct (now called Bethel Hill) – Washington Township
- *Elias Plew* – Pleasant View Cemetery – East of Dover
- *Jesse Robertson* – Hopewell – North of Lebanon on Highway 47
- *John Roberts* – Mechanicsburg Cemetery – Mechanicsburg
- *Abraham Utter* – Cox Cemetery – Thorntown/ Northwest of Dover
- *John Wheatler* – Private – East of Lebanon
- *Joseph Wheatley* – Hixson Farm – Private property, Union Township (sometimes referred to as Norwood Cemetery)

Visiting Relatives: Tips for Cemetery Visits for Genealogists

∽

My family tree has many branches, both living and dead... but all equally important. I cherish the memories that make its roots run deep." (Lynda I Fisher)

For me, visiting bygone relatives usually means getting down and dirty. I think cemeteries are a tranquil, fascinating place. So many lives, so many stories untold–so much history we might otherwise miss! As a Family Historian, going relative hunting is one of my favorite adventures.

I've done this grave hunting thing all over the place. On vacations I've wandered around above-ground crypts built inside the below-sea-level cemeteries of New Orleans. Visiting Louisville I've plopped down to have a rest on the jutting-up end of a vault because it was the closest thing to a level spot around. Nearer to home, I once spent a long snowy afternoon chatting with a gentle herd of dairy cows while traversing acres of laid-over winter wheat. My field companions were searching leisurely for snacks; I was looking for a lonely plot.

There is little I love more than crisp autumn colors next to bleached-out marble. Except, maybe a majestic lawn of showy statuary at a big beautiful graveyard.

Nope, it doesn't creep me out.

Yes, I guess that's a little nutty.

The point is–I've done a lot of this field-stalking for the graves of forefathers, and in my travels I've learned some really good tips and tricks. Sure there are lots more "do's and don'ts" but this is my standard list of rules, go-to methods, and handy stuff to drag along.

Finding an old grave can be a challenge, but if you hang with it, you're bound to make a discovery or two worth your while.

So here are my "rules" for visiting, and some handy-to-have stuff to take along. I hope you'll take time to try some hunting yourself, and then let me know how it panned out for you and your kin!

RULES

1. MANY cemeteries in Boone County are on private property; especially the defunct ones. Some are even on folk's lawns–very close to their house. Often, these properties are owned by easily startled seniors. No matter who lives there, be respectful. Do not stomp up next to someone's home and start taking pictures of a little plot sectioned-off with some pretty iron fencing.

2. For visits on private property with no public access right-of-way (common) drop a courtesy note in the mailbox of the occupant well in advance of your site visit. State your business, and ask for permission to come by *at their convenience* to take a look. Respect their wishes. Please describe your vehicle, ask before photographing, and give them all of your contact information. You may discover you're cousins!

3. Take notes of your visits. Record the who, what, when, why, how and what I should remember to do/bring next time. Be sure to carry your notes at all times.

STUFF to TAKE — THINGS to DO

Here are my best tips for a successful trip to any cemetery for ancestor hunting. These can be especially important to heed if you're setting off for a very old, defunct, or out-of-the-way location.

- *Make a list of who you are looking for, and where they are buried ahead of time.* You can use the spaces next to cemetery names in this book to jot down some notes, or make your own dedicated notebook. Most places (remember to check for additional site names when more than one is noted) can be found with the mapping or GPS feature online at Find A Grave. This is a free site and a great resource for searching.
- *While you're on Find A Grave* sign up to be a contributor. This is a kindness to others, especially for those "out of the way" or special-permission-needed sites. Take your time and get a good face-on photo of all the legible markers you can. Upload the photos to the cemetery's listing later. It's a nice way to return the favor of the images you've found on that webpage of your own family.
- *Whenever possible, take a companion.* This is good advice anytime you start an adventure.
- *Also take along a bag* with a large towel or heavy blanket, a flashlight, your notebook and pen, any emergency medications you might need (inhaler, nitro tablets, Epi-pen etc), a spray bottle filled with distilled water, a few old toothbrushes, some sturdy gloves, a small roll of aluminum foil, some kitchen shears heavy enough to cut through vines. Oh, and personally I do love a super

sturdy trash bag to put between me and nature as I sit and kneel in the mud, bugs, and weedy grass.

- *Always make a note of where your car is parked* in your records during each trip (what entry point did you use?). No, I don't think you'll get lost, but it will be of use to you later when you are mapping sites and recording the position of certain graves.

- *Never step out of your car without taking along a fully charged cellphone.* In case of emergency–and lots of emergencies can happen–this simple tool can really save you!

- *Have your camera on-hand and ready.* Carry spare batteries or be sure it is fully charged. If you will be using your cell phone's camera, be sure it's set for high performance with the automatic flash turned off. If you don't know how to set up your phone to do its best picture taking, stop by a retailer and have a sales tech do it for you. Digital photos are the best tool for reading old stones.

- *Take a large stick with you.* Though you may not have to fight back bears, you may stumble upon a snake or other critter. I'd rather shoo away a curious groundhog with a long stick than my camera bag any day! Also, uneven ground is a given–especially in graveyards with the oldest interments. Count on them to be riddled with animal burrows, large roots, broken off stones and sunken spots. All of these can easily cause a fall or a broken bone. Use your stick as a "leading leg" to test the ground before you. Although it may seem awkward at first, once you get the hang of it, you'll wonder how you ever did without!

- *Be sure to keep your eyes and ears keen to your surroundings.* Lock your car. Be on the look-out for thieves or feisty Hobos. Also, hornets, or ground bees, seem to adore living in old cemeteries. If you hear their hum, just steer clear of them and you will *all* have a better day.

- *Wear a hat if you'd like,* but be sure to remove it, or turn it backward before taking photos. The shade of the brim or bill can affect the automatic light level detection on today's cameras and cause a lesser quality image.

- *Long pants, boots or sturdy shoes, bug spray and long-sleeved shirts are a great defense against ticks and biting insects or poison ivy rashes.*
- *Once you've found who you're looking for (especially in large graveyards) make yourself a little map.* Remember how you noted where you left the car? Now is the time to use that. Photograph the grave marker so the name and shape are clear. Then, stand at the grave with your back to your parked vehicle (make a habit of beginning from this position). At eye level, take a photo. Make a clockwise quarter turn, and take another. Keep going until you have an image of what you see in all four directions when you are standing graveside. Digital photography rocks! This 4-way-shot of the site will help lead you or others on the next visit.
- *Visually inspect the stone/marker for signs of dangerous deterioration.* Look each stone over before touching it. Watch for chipping, cracks, breaks, previous repairs, crumbling, or any open-grain or sandy spots. Be warned that even the thinnest upright markers can be very heavy and cause some serious damage if they "snap" while you're nicely wiping moss away. Safety first!
- *When you encounter old, very faded stones that are not quite legible, then a companion's extra set of hands will come in really handy.* Using the blanket or large towel to shade the tombstone, prop your flashlight onto the bottom edge of the grave-marker. Without a flash, take a close photo while under the shade of the cloth. Then try shining the flashlight downward on the faint markings (while still keeping it, the camera and the stone shaded from sunlight). The results may not be immediately apparent, but at home with some simple editing features found on

most cameras and phones, you might unveil the
previously invisible.

- *Do check the sides, back and top edge of each stone as well as
  the front.* Occasionally you will find surprises like
  fraternal emblems or an ornamental symbol carved in the
  stone. Compare any findings like these to the exhaustive
  list available on the AGS website (address below). These
  may generate a new clue to your relative's "earthly"
  interests.
- *If the surface is obscured by weeds or dirt, cut away the
  vegetation with the kitchen shears.* Mud and dirt deposits,
  along with any grass overgrowth on flat stones should be
  peeled off by hand (use the gloves if you'd like). Lichens
  and moss often plague markers in shady areas. Use a dry
  toothbrush to gently scrub them away. If you need a little
  more help, spritz the area with distilled water and allow it
  to soften the crud. Then, using a light touch, wipe it
  away with a towel or toothbrush.
- *Wetting the face of a stone with water is another trick for
  reading barely-there etchings.* Be sure to try photographing
  the tough-to-read ones both wet and dry.
- *Occasionally, you can get a good result by laying aluminum
  foil (shiny side down) over the epitaph and lightly rubbing it
  with your hands.* Once you've done your best, photograph
  the stone again with the foil still in place. Carefully set
  the embossed foil sheet aside to reexamine at home.
- *Think you have a great method for how to clean/read/repair a
  gravestone?* You may have heard shaving cream, baby
  powder, cornstarch or all purpose flour is the easy way to
  read old stones. Although each one sounds harmless
  enough, don't do it! Check in with the AGS website first
  (the Association for Gravestone Studies). These folks
  know their stuff and are up-to-date on what does and
  does not cause harm to these precious relics. Find their

fascinating, info-rich website
at https://gravestonestudies.org

- *My newest favorite "must-have-toy"* for any Family History
  expedition is a GoPro-type camera. These little digital
  devices allow you to make incredible videos; effortlessly
  documenting your outing complete with sound. By
  simply mounting the GoPro onto your hat or wearing an
  accessory headband you can record your adventure. This
  is SO helpful to review when trying to clarify notes once
  you've returned home to your computer. I highly
  recommend investing in one, especially if you will be
  traveling to a place you may only have one shot at seeing
  (a Black Forest graveyard, a bike tour across your county
  of origin in Ireland, a crumbling farmstead in back-
  country Georgia).

- *And, Indiana-Boone-Jones, if you think you've found a
  previously undocumented grave site, be sure to contact the
  nearest health department to inform them of your discovery.*

You just might make the papers!

List of Boone Cemeteries and Gravesites

"Our dead are never dead to us, until we have forgotten them."
(George Eliot)

About 100 small burial sites and assorted-size cemeteries are documented in the State of Boone. Although the earliest interment of a white settler seems to have gone unrecorded, he or she was likely buried near their homestead or taken back to their previous hometown to be buried alongside family.

More than a few have been lost to time.

For years, Boone was pure wilderness; not a tillable, gentrified land. Marshy ground was eager to assist Mother Nature's claim on our ancestors. In the early years when survival was a daily struggle, this place of hardship left little time for sentiment. Early graves in the county were often marked with home-carved slabs of sandstone, wide boards or simple wood crosses.

Surprisingly, before 1999, there were no laws prohibiting crop raising or livestock grazing over known grave sites. For years, common decency (via reverence for the dead) was left in the hands of those who farmed and settled near old graves. Although some heartless types chose to discard markers of long abandoned graves, many folks plowed or built over all sorts of cemeteries without knowing.

Here is a list compiled from several sources–both antiquated and modern–of burials within our borders. Where a place has been known by multiple names, I've listed all the alternates alphabetically in a group.

Important:

Before you go field stalking for forefathers, see the chapter *Visiting Relatives* so you'll be prepared, welcomed–and will cause no harm.

———————

Beck (Lebanon)

———————

Beck – Demaree – Muncey (Advance)

———————

Beeler – Harman – Marsh – Pitzer (Zionsville)

———————

Bethel (Pike)

———————

Bethel – Clarkston – Clarkstown (Zionsville)

———————

Bethel Hill – Precinct (Lebanon)

———————

Bethel – Wright (Waugh)

———————

Big Springs – Richardson (Big Springs)

———————

Bishop – Zionsville (Zionsville)

———————

Brockway (Max)

———————

Brown (New Ross)

———————

Brown's Wonder (Lebanon)

———————

Brush Creek (Thorntown)

———————

Cason (Hazelrigg)

———————

Cedar Hill – Old City (Lebanon)

———————

Center (Lebanon)

———————

Chitwood (Harrison Twp)

———————

Clarkston – Clarkstown – Bethel (Zionsville)

———————

Clarkstown – Bethel – Clarkston (Zionsville)

———————

Clements – Pratt (Jackson Twp)

———————

Colored Cemetery (Thorntown)

———————

County Farm – Pauper's – Poor Farm
    Potter's Field (Lebanon)

———————

Cox (Dover)

———————

Cox – Old Eagle (Zionsville)

———————

Curry (Thorntown)

———————

Dale – Squire Dale (Jamestown)

———————

Demaree – Muncey – Beck (Advance)

———————

Dickerson (Fayette)

———————

Dover (Dover)

———————

Dowden (Lebanon)

———————

Eagle Creek Regular Baptist (Eagle Village)

———————

Eagle Village (Eagle Village)

———————

Elizaville (Elizaville)

———————

Garret (Mechanicsburg)

———————

Gipson (Thorntown)

———————

Green (Thorntown)

———————

Harmon – Marsh – Pitzer – Beeler (Zionsville)

———————

Heckathron (Jackson Twp)

———————

Herndon – Hostetter (Dover)

———————

Howard (Fayette)

———————

Howard (Jamestown)

———————

Hutton Memorial – Pleasant View East (Northview)

———————

Independent Order of Odd Fellows (Jamestown)

———————

Jamestown IOOF (Jamestown)

———————

Jemima Harness (Thorntown)

———————

Johns (Big Springs)

———————

Johns Family (Thorntown)

———————

Jones (Zionsville)

———————

Jones – Parr (Big Springs)

———————

Joseph Wheatly – Wheatly (Union Twp)

———————

Kirklin Pioneer (Terhune)

———————

Lane (Northfield)

———————

Lincoln Memory Gardens (Whitestown)

———————

Lockman (Advance)

———————

Lowry (Jamestown)

———————

Lutheran – Old Lutheran (Whitestown)

———————

Maple Lawn*** (Thorntown)

———————

Marsh – Pitzer – Beeler – Harmon (Zionsville)

———————

McCord (Whitestown)

———————

Mechanicsburg (Mechanicsburg)

———————

Miami Indian – Old Indian (Thorntown)

———————

Milledgeville (Milledgeville)

———————

Moore (Elizaville)

———————

Mount Tabor – Mt Tabor (Fayette)

———————

Mount Union (Milledgeville)

———————

Mount Zion (Jamestown)

———————

Mounts Run – Mts Run (Whitestown)

———————

Mt Tabor – Mount Tabor (Fayette)

———————

Mts Run – Mounts Run (Whitestown)

———————

Mud Creek – Salem (Elizaville)

———————

Muncey – Beck – Demaree (Advance)

———————

Newby (Marion Twp)

———————

Oak Hill – Rodefer (Lebanon)

———————

Old Bethel – Old Clarkston – Old Clarkstown (Zionsville)

———————

Old City – Cedar Hill (Lebanon)

———————

Old Clarkston – Old Clarkstown – Old Bethel (Zionsville)

———————

Old Clarkstown – Old Bethel – Old Clarkston (Zionsville)

———————

Old Eagle – Cox (Zionsville)

———————

Old Harmon (Eagle Village)

———————

Old Indian – Miami Indian (Thorntown)

———

Old Lutheran – Lutheran (Whitestown)

———

Old Mt Zion (Max)

———

Old Thorntown – Thorntown (Thorntown)

———

Old Union Church – Union (Jamestown)

———

Parr – Jones (Big Springs)

———

Pauper's – Poor Farm – Potter's Farm –
    County Farm (Lebanon)

———

Pitzer – Beeler – Harmon – Beeler (Zionsville)

———

Pleasant View (Dover)

———

Pleasant View East – Hutton Memorial (Northfield)

———

Poor Farm – County Farm – Pauper's –
    Potter's Field (Lebanon)

———

Poor Farm – Potter's Field – Pauper's –
    County Farm (Lebanon)

———

Poplar Grove (New Brunswick)

———

Porter (Jamestown)

_____

Potter's Field – County Farm –
    Pauper's – Poor Farm (Lebanon)

_____

Pratt – Clements (Jackson Twp)

_____

Precinct – Bethel Hill (Lebanon)

_____

Richardson – Big Springs (Big Springs)

_____

Robinson (Lebanon)

_____

Rodefer – Oak Hill (Lebanon)

_____

Rosston (Rosston)

_____

Salem (Zionsville)

_____

Salem – Mud Creek (Elizaville)

_____

Schooler (Eagle Twp)

_____

Sedwick – Segwick (Wurster Lake*)

_____

Sedwick – Simeon (Girl Scout Camp**)

_____

Segwick – Sedwick (Wurster Lake*)

_____

Sheets (Zionsville)

———————

Shepard – Shepherd (Mechanicsburg)

———————

Shepherd – Sheparp (Mechanicsburg)

———————

Simeon – Sedwick (Girl Scout Camp**)

———————

Smith – Thornley (Fayette)

———————

Spicklemire (Harrison Twp)

———————

Squire Dale – Dale (Jamestown)

———————

St Francis of the Fields Episcopal Columbarium
    (Zionsville)

———————

St Joseph Catholic (Lebanon)
    (in oldest records appears as St Joachim)

———————

Sugar Plains (Thorntown)

———————

Taylor (Hazelrigg)

———————

Thornley – Smith (Fayette)

———————

Thorntown – Old Thorntown (Thorntown)

———————

Trotter (Jamestown)

Union – Old Union Church (Jamestown)

Unmarked – near Bethel (Big Springs)

Unmarked – Shepherdsville Road (Herr)

Walnut Grove (Thorntown)

Wheatly – Joseph Wheatly (Union Twp)

Wright – Bethel (Waugh)

Zionsville – Bishop (Zionsville)

*Wurster Lake is near Rosston

**Girl Scout Camp is privately owned, near Rosston. You must have written permission and an escort to visit.

***One instance was found of Maple Lawn being referred to as "New Cemetery." Perhaps because it was the new alternative to the quickly filling Thorntown / Old Thorntown graveyard within town limits. Maple Lawn was also reported to have had several "mounds" on its property, although I found no evidence of ancient or Indian burials being either discovered or disturbed there.

Did You Know?

Around 1870 many optimistic folks discussed the possibility of Lebanon replacing Indianapolis as the State Capital.

In 1871 an enthusiastic opinion piece was printed by *The Lebanon Pioneer*. Editor BA Smith proclaimed the removal of the state capital from Indianapolis to Lebanon as just shy of a sure-fire-done-deal. Smith crowed the excellent event-to-be was an upcoming byproduct of the recently announced railway connecting Anderson, Lebanon and St Louis.

Hopes for an economic and status upsurge declined as the lauded railway failed to materialize. Then, three years later in 1874, Indianapolis announced its original city limits would require expansion outward to encompass the entirety of Marion County's Center Township. The already-named capital city south of Lebanon was exploding with industry and population; benefiting from its place as the crossroads of America.

The blustering talk of Lebanon as the new capital of Indiana deflated to a whimper. The golden glory promised by the Anderson, Lebanon & St Louis remained mired in a tangle of problems. Not a bit of its anticipated prosperity had crossed into Boone County since it was first announced. Finally after sixteen years of bankruptcy, receivership and changing of hands, the be-all, end-all railway arrived; made-over as the Midland Line.

Not long after it was up and running, the Midland earned a dubious nickname that stuck– "Indiana's Most Unsuccessful Railway." Today, a wide alley running across the center of Oak Hill Cemetery and some abandoned tracks straddled by the town of Advance are the most noticeable relics of the ill-fated Midland.

*

Just because no one has ever been full-on hanged in Boone County doesn't mean that pioneer hearts were full-up with shining rainbows and prancing unicorn ponies.

Early Boone County wasn't immune to the plague of crime, disagreement, unlawful actions or general wildness. Like any other startup civilization, Boone has a history marred with its share of dark times and questionable moments.

Rumors still swirl of long-ago lynchings in Boone County. Historic Holiday Bridge (aka Hundred Foot Bridge) in rural Zionsville is believed by many to be the site of a KKK perpetrated lynching of two innocent black travelers from its old iron trestles. However, lots of folks smarter than me have searched and re-searched and have found no evidence that *anyone* has ever swung from the framework.

The most cited event is the "almost hanged" case of Frank Hall on the courthouse square (see *Mary Mary Mary* for the full scoop). In years of telling and retelling, people have heard bits of the story and then concluded that Hall was indeed hanged from a tree on the courthouse lawn. Some even insist that because of Hall's lynching, trees are no longer allowed on Lebanon's Square. Folks' ears naturally perk up when they hear about a lynch mob. Then it's easy to be bored by the details and assume the angry rabble completed its mission.

*

An 1896 report of "White Cap" justice was made in Boone County, but was likely a put-on show.

The hooded group paid a late night visit at the home of a widowed man who lived with his daughter. Boarding with them was a young man named Marion Kendall. The residence was an unlikely target for a group such as the KKK. All occupants of the home were white, born stateside, and protestant by faith.

Mounted White Caps with blazing torches summoned Kendall from his rented room in the house. They proceeded to tie him to a tree and where they bludgeoned and whipped him brutally before heaving him back into the house. Upon scrutiny of the incident, officials later speculated that the whole thing was a set up. Rumors circulated that Kendall had made advances on his host's daughter.

Kendall insisted he was innocent of any wrong doing. He held to his claim that the girl's errantly angry father was the main schemer of the night visit.

After barely surviving the attack, recovery from the beating at a local rest home was slow. Marion Kendall was left paralyzed. He filed suit. In it, he named several "high profile" citizens of the county, claiming he'd recognized them during the attack. Kendall sought $10,000 damages. After four years of trials and appeals, the Indiana Supreme Court decided in his favor. In 1900 he was awarded half of what he originally demanded. The five thousand dollars Kendall received was equivalent to a $60,000 settlement in 2016 money.

*

A KKK funeral was held in Lebanon and captured in a photograph...or was it?

In 1923 a specialty newspaper pressed in Indianapolis known as *The Fiery Cross* published a photograph of Kirklin resident Grace Powell being buried at Lebanon's Oak Hill Cemetery. The article further described her as a member of the Elizaville Christian Church with services conducted by Reverend HN Vandervort. The photo shows a sizable group of women in hoods and robes at the open grave site performing traditional funeral rituals of the Ku Klux Klan. *The Fiery Cross* said that Mrs Powell had previously lived in Boone County, but was residing across the county line in Kirklin at the time of her passing. No record of interment exists at Oak Hill for a Grace Powell.

*

Jamestown, original and some say rightful capital of The State
of Boone, can claim bragging rights for another of Boone
County's "firsts."

The death of Noah Johnson became the first-ever murder case
on Boone County soil. The whole thing happened right on Main
Street in the generally docile town. Divergent philosophical
points-of-view instigated what ended with a tragic result. In 1840
on a cool Thursday evening in November, a pair of gentlemen
began arguing over politics. Upstanding businessman Patrick
Slatery (popular local storekeeper) was verbally tussling with the
less sophisticated local, Noah H Johnson.

Slatery, overwhelmed by the frustration of Johnson's refusal
to agree, got physical. Grabbing a nearby club (clubs were always
at-hand in the good old days), Mr Slatery landed it squarely over
Mr Johnson's hard head. In the heat of the moment, this action
seemed to be the best solution to pound some much-needed sense
into Johnson.

The following afternoon, Noah Johnson died from a fractured
skull. Coroner John Lawrence convened an investigative jury on
Saturday; less than 48 hours after the fight. With so few residents,
justice could be swift.

Six eyewitnesses appeared to speak their viewpoint of that
evening's unfortunate altercation. Most of those testifying were
friends of, and sided with, the popular merchant. The pool of
jurors generally agreed that some people just needed a good
whack to the head. In researching the Jamestown incident, it
appears Patrick Slatery had a lot of friends. He was neither tried
nor convicted.

*

Perry Township was known for years as Bloody Perry;
especially when it came to politics.

Stories still circulate today about the Horse Thief Detectives
Association and the vigilante-style law enforcement and vote-

persuasion the little township was famed for. In that corner of the county, if you weren't a Democrat, you were better off relocating.

In the interest of author disclosure–I'm sorta related to an officer or two of that Horse Thief Detectives outfit.

"Whoopsy"

Although most of the Horse Thief Detectives were level-headed citizens who took upholding the law as a sacred oath to be followed squarely by the letter and spirit; others got a little drunk with power. Some of the units (each organized group was considered a separate unit from the others, though under the same umbrella) went a little off-mission.

Some, in fact, were loaded with members who were also White Cap Avengers (akin to the Ku Klux Klan) or other "law in our own hands" types. Even today in some circles, a story is told about a certain mid-ranking Horse Thief Detective who was actually more horse thief than detective. What a perfect fox-in-the-hen-house situation!

If you are curious about your own roots in Boone, you may want to take a look at the officer listing on the next pages. Taken from the official roll call at a 1920s era state convention held in nearby Frankfort, many surnames are familiar. With all the vigilante tough guys in attendance, perhaps you'll find yourself claiming a familial Whoopsy too!

*

Fighting lines were drawn for more than politics in tiny Perry township. And it wasn't just the criminally disposed who found a seat in the courthouse.

For three or four years, a church at the edge of Fayette was so deeply embroiled in theological infighting that the matter was brought before the Indiana Supreme Court.

In 1889 the congregation of Mount Tabor Regular (Primitive) Baptist church was constantly simmering in preparation for an all-out brawl. A majority of the membership favored a new idea–preaching the Gospel would quicken dead sinners into spiritual life.

The premise sounded harmless enough, however, the "dead sinners" targeted were among the founders of Mt Tabor. Related to many still-alive members, the dead sinners were tucked peacefully into tidy graves beside the modest church. According to the doctrine Mt Tabor was founded on, their souls had already been ushered directly to their heavenly reward.

Saying that the departed members needed a "boost" to reach Heaven was both appalling and insulting to the older (but by then, minority) members.

A war of words, fiery speeches, and a few fist-a-cuffs followed as the two factions, old and new, sought to control ownership of the building, grounds and the right to determine Mt Tabor's theological future.

Though the scrap began sometime during 1889, it wasn't concluded (at least in the eyes of the law) until a decision was handed down from the Supreme Court in 1893. On March 15th, the Primitives won. The court ruled that a church's property belonged to those who founded it, and that it would continue under their intentions and beliefs until those founders decided otherwise.

Even the Supreme Court knew no good could come from a coup that forced folks to change horses midstream…especially the one horse folks spent their earthly life with intentions of riding straight to heaven.

*

As the Civil War was raging, Boone County, and much of Indiana, was still a dangerously lawless new frontier.

One day in 1865, a local farmer was kidnapped off his own property. In a remote part of Marion Township, about one mile north of where highways 47 and 52 cross, was the new farm of Samuel Titus. On an early spring morning during the second year that Sam and his wife inhabited their land, he was accosted by a band of unfriendly Indians.

Encircling Titus, they captured him and led him away bound and gagged. The Indians took Titus to the place where they were at camp. They threw their captive to the ground near the warmth of the fire but gave him no food or water. The site was only an overnight stop as they moved along to their summer hunting place.

In the morning he was untied and led to the cooking fire. Braves were seated in a circle watching as an old chief smoked a long pipe. A kettle tended by a squaw simmered at the center. Soon a bowl of broth dipped up from the pot was passed around the circle. Starting with the chief, each man was given a turn using a communal spoon. Sam was wary of what might be served as breakfast by savages.

On the first passing of the bowl, he raised the spoon to his lips only pretending to sip the broth. When the bowl was refilled and passed again, Titus dipped the spoon to the bottom and raised up a dog's leg still covered in fur.

For the next several days Sam tried to live off of grass and berries as the tribe kept moving toward their summer encampment. Finally, hunger overwhelmed his repulsion and he became willing to eat anything presented in the shared bowl.

The party was constantly traveling. Titus was forced to walk along the uneven forest trails with his hands bound behind him. At night, they tied his feet together as well and put him between two braves to sleep. Sam watched constantly for any chance to escape. Reaching their large summer hunting ground, he was allowed to move about camp more freely but was always watched. His hands remained bound at his back.

Weeks passed into months. The tribe began preparations to move again. They were breaking camp to head south to their fall place where the weather would be milder. By then, poor Samuel was convinced he would never find an opportunity to get away from his captors. He'd lost hope of ever returning home to his wife and four children.

Before the Indians completed preparations for their

southward migration, the chief summonsed Titus. The leader told Sam he was a good man because he had not attempted to escape. This, the chief reasoned, had earned him an opportunity to be set free. He motioned for six of his braves to come join Titus and himself. The braves stripped Sam of his shirt and unbound his wrists. Telling the farmer that if he wished to be freed he would have to be faster than the tribe's best warriors, the chief shoved Titus toward the forest, ordering him to run. About 100 yards away from the fire, Sam heard the whoop of braves beginning to pursue him.

One young warrior caught up to Sam and took aim with his tomahawk. In a stroke of luck, the Indian tripped on the heavy brush and fell flat onto his face. Titus spun around and grabbed the weapon from the brave's hand; splitting the aggressor's skull wide open.

Coming upon their injured friend, the other braves paused to examine his wound. This gave Titus the break he needed to reach the river before them. He ran out onto a log jam and jumped into the dark water beneath. Sam stayed in the debris pack hidden among snakes and turtles for what seemed like hours until the warriors gave up and turned back to camp.

At nightfall, Titus floated downstream looking for a safe place to come out of the water. After about a mile he found a patch of bank covered in gravel where he would leave no footprints. Estimating that he was northwest of his home he ran in a southeasterly direction using the stars to guide him. Sam spent the next week traveling across the countryside; again eating only foraged foods like grass and tender roots. He slept inside hollow trees, or under the cover of brush. After seven days he came upon a settler's cabin in a clearing.

The kind inhabitants took pity and invited him in. They gave him his first real meal in months. The couple told him he was about a day's journey north of the large settlement called Lafayette. From there, Samuel knew it would only be another 30 miles to his home.

From Lafayette, he traveled an old Indian path running from the Wabash to the White River. He knew the path well; it cut across the edge of his own farm.

This path was later used to layout the Indianapolis Road (highway 52).

After months of ordeal, Samuel Titus was back at his home. It's said he walked up the lane toward his house, casually whistling his favorite tune.

*

Although not as epic as the tale of Sam Titus, another Boone County kidnapping in Dover shook residents to their core.

In the 1930s John and Laura Utley bought the old Bennington store in town. The young couple worked hard and remodeled the place with upgrades to the building and grounds. Riding the wave of modernization, they installed a pair of mechanical gasoline pumps in front of the business.

One day Laura walked into the store after an errand. She was confused when she saw a stranger standing at the cash register. Her husband John was nowhere in sight. Shock set in when she realized the stranger held a revolver in one hand while pulling money out of the drawer with the other.

The bandit saw Laura and raised his gun at her. He commanded her to stay still. Holding a steady aim on the terrified young woman, the man pushed past her, running out the door to the waiting get-away car. As they pulled away, she saw her husband John riding in the back seat with a gun held to his head.

Overwhelmed with fear, Laura immediately called for both the county sheriff and the Horse Thief Detectives. With special privileges granted under the law, members of the HTDA were authorized to cross county and state lines in pursuit of major criminals.

While the lawmen searched, the robbers drove recklessly along country roads; crisscrossing county lines and holding a gun firmly in John Utley's side. Several hours later, the kidnappers unceremoniously slowed the car and dumped their captive outside of Lebanon without even coming to a full stop.

After a long walk, John Utley found a telephone and was able to alert authorities and his wife that he'd been turned loose and was unharmed. The men who had robbed and abducted him were never caught.

*

During the years leading up to the Civil War, especially at Royalton and all areas surrounding Whitestown, the Copperhead movement had a foothold.

A Copperhead was a northerner sympathetic and supportive of the Confederacy. Other organized factions in the area held with the same loyalties. The Knights of the Golden Circle and the Butternuts were heavily entrenched, counting many loyal members around Union and Worth townships.

One of the treasonous groups met weekly in an open field near Royalton for muster and drilling exercises. They did this in preparation for the coming glory of their big moment. Another met at an abandoned cabin outside of Fayette to plot strategy, exchange intelligence and catch up with news of the larger network of anti-Union ideologies. The third group of schemers acted as an information pipeline working with like-minded citizens in adjoining communities.

The three groups held up the general hope that their anti-Union bands could overthrow Governor Morton; thus adding Indiana to the role-call of the Confederacy.

During sign-ups and accounting of able bodied men available for drafting into Union service, a mini-coup occurred. An enrolling officer assigned to Whitestown in June of 1863 was met with Copperhead opposition. Army intelligence reports estimated the Copperhead membership at somewhere between 100 and 150 in the small town of 400 residents.

The enrollment officer sent word of his difficulties back to commanders at Indianapolis. Immediately a group of 50 soldiers under Captain Holloway was dispatched. Strategically coming to the outskirts of Whitestown under the cover of darkness, they bivouacked overnight sending scouts ahead. The reconnaissance men found the small city closely guarded by sentinels on each corner. With effort, the scouts were able to slip around the guards. Word of the army presence was passed to a few trusted citizens who were part of the Home Guard.

With the help from loyalists living within Whitestown's borders, Holloway's men walked into town the next morning at an early hour. They began going door-to-door escorting the enrollment officer. Most folks responded by polite compliance (no doubt taken by surprise in their long-johns and nightclothes). Enrollment was completed with little threat of bloodshed.

Although most of the Union disinters responded peacefully, Copperhead William George took off running. One of Holloway's troops fired at George as he fled. It is doubtful that George was hit as he was able to escape. Fourteen men who refused to enroll were taken into custody and transported by train to Indianapolis to face charges. A sizable cache of firearms was also collected.

By 9am Captain Holloway's mission was complete. The morning was considered a huge success. Two suspected Copperheads even enlisted on the spot fearing later repercussions.

While researching, I found a few names noted in one or more written sources who were alleged to be Copperheads, Butternuts, or Knights of the Golden Circle (some held multiple memberships). I've added them for your review a few pages after this chapter.

*

North of Lebanon, the tiny settlement known as Ratsburg wasn't always a picnic either.

The road into Ratsburg was great–if you were a ravenously hungry grasshopper. In late summer, 1869 the remains of an unfortunate traveler were found in a ditch. The man had been attacked and eaten alive by a massive cloud of the destructive insects. His body was never identified or claimed. Swarms of grasshoppers menaced the Midwest and Plains States during the entire growing season that year.

*

Copperheads, Butternuts and Golden Knights

⁗⁓∞⁓⁗

Here are the names I ran across while researching the *Whitestown Enrollment Rebellion*. Several men were openly known as members of one or all of the treasonous organizations involved. Even though their affiliations were indeed considered as Treason, and thus among the vilest of crimes, those who were brought to justice faced little penalty. I found no record of any of these men receiving more than a fine, a short stay in jail, or a combo of the two punishments. Our government of the time must have understood basic beliefs couldn't easily be categorized by circumstances of simple geography.

Conrad Hill, Nathan Curtis, James M Lucas, Francis Sanders, William Brandenburg, Jonathan Hall, Jim Wilson, Jim Crane, John Doyle, Nettie Doyle, Jeremiah Gleeson, John Douglass, Eli Goodwin, Johnny Howard, John Cox, Anderson Lewis, Patrick Lee, Patrick White, Jeremiah Nichols, John Nichols, Jacob Hill, Wright Sims, William P Clements

National Horse Thief Dectective Association

Following is an alphabetical list of the registered Companies of the NHTDA in Boone County and the men who served as officers of each. The list comes from a state convention held in Frankfort Indiana during the 1920s. Some interesting stats are included in the original document. Elizaville, being Company 16, was the county's oldest charter and also one of the first in the state. Eagle Company of Zionsville boasted the most Boone County members at 164. Lebanon was next highest with 73 active members. Membership in Thorntown's Company counted only 14 Horse Thief Detectives.

Eagle #25 164 members
Wm A Schofield, President
Pirtel N Shaw, Secretary
Wm A Wood, Captain

Elizaville #16   23 members
Earnest Sample, President
Roy Sample, Secretary
Otis McRoberts, Captain

Fayette #247   34 members
TC Beasley, President
Lester E Everett, Secretary
DT Shepherd, Captain

Gadsden #124   60 members
BL Smiley, President
WE Essex, Secretary
AE Hine, Captain

Jamestown #47   44 members
WS Cortney, President
Arthur Joseph, Secretary
Milt Skaggs, Captain

Jefferson #149   21 members
BL Sumpter, President
Sherman Gregory, Secretary
Roy Wiley, Captain

Lebanon #127   73 members
RC Holmes, President
John W Fulwider, Secretary
R Holmes, Captain

Mechanicsburg #26   39 members
JA Blubaugh, President

Cheslie B Lough, Secretary
Dr GM Blubaugh, Captain

New Brunswick #71   22 members
MG Kimmel, President
GH Robertson, Secretary
Roy Northcutt, Captain

North Eel River #340   58 members
Buel Dale, President
Walter Moore, Secretary
Ed Davis, Captain

Thorntown #45   14 members
Arrel Holmes, President
Arthur P Hammel, Secretary
Charles Stout, Captain

Whitestown #139   38 members
MJ Miller, President
John H Groover, Secreary
Walter Schooler, Captain

The program of the annual meeting lists each county in Indiana. If you are working on a Family History outside of Boone County and are curious whether or not there are members in your tree, please feel free to contact me. I would be happy to share another county's listing with you!

Pioneer Doctors

"It cannot be said that our early doctors were all men of eminent scientific skill or training. Few of them held diplomas from medical colleges, for 70 to 80 years ago medical colleges were not as thick in the land as they are now." (Dr George McCoy quoted c. 1910)

Before the Civil War, only a handful of colleges offered medical degrees in the United States. In those times, it was common to apprentice with an established physician for three years to learn doctoring. Those who trained in this method were considered Regular or Allopathic doctors. Collegiate medical training in the United States was purely elective. The four colleges in the US with medical schools were merely two-year stopovers after completing an apprenticeship for those who could afford it. To attend college specifically for physician or surgical training Americans had to enroll in schools abroad. Understandably, most took the more accessible route via apprenticeship.

In order to apprentice, Doctor-Wannabes paid an annual fee and agreed to do menial chores in exchange for training alongside an established practitioner. For three years, the trainee observed the daily life and case-load of a pioneer-time physician.

When war broke out between the north and south, some young men enlisted as farm-boys and returned home with a new career. For many, their service as medics assisting field surgeons qualified them as doctors. Battlefields and the conditions of war presented an excellent track for learning.

The founder of Boone County's first hospital–or Surgical Institute– was James (J.F.L.) Garrison. Although records of Hartsville University (now Huntington University in Bartholomew County) indicate Garrison was enrolled during the 1850s, no record is available showing how long he attended, or whether he was granted a diploma in any discipline.

His army career began when he enlisted as a private in December of 1861 in the light artillery/ battery division. Records of Garrison's second enlistment in October 1863 show him as an "Assistant Surgeon." His military career concluded in 1865 at war's end after achieving the rank and title Major/Surgeon.

With a postwar flood of practicing doctors, the field of medicine became more competitive. Training schools began springing up. Few were tied to Universities. Teaching hospitals as we know them now, wouldn't exist for three or four more decades.

Most women in medicine were nurses. Many signed up for on-the-job training and were required to live in dormitories attached to the hospitals. Any female wishing to become a doctor or surgeon had to find a private practice mentor willing to take her on as an apprentice.

A survey by the 1885 Indiana Department of Health shows that Boone County, with its population of about 32,000 was rather modern in physician gender. Of the 55 listed as practicing that year in our county, at least two were female.

Not wanting to miss the financial opportunity, more and more established Universities began offering dedicated two year courses. The application and acceptance policy was generally rooted in "ability to pay." However, the student's name on a State University diploma carried more prestige than a surgical institute with a shingle above the local druggist's storefront on the town square–or none at all.

In these years, all curriculum was modeled after the early American colleges which offered two year studies in medicine. First year students typically spent two identical four-month sessions hearing lectures for eight hours daily on core subjects. Supplemental readings were assigned each night, but were not mandatory. Exams were pretty optional too.

In this time, discipline issues were rampant–however expulsion was uncommon. The consequences for ill-behavior or sub-par attendance were all financial. Negligent or naughty students were fined, then reinstated once they had paid up.

To say the curriculum was fairly scant may be one of the broadest understatements ever. The material presented second semester (2nd session) was identical to the class lectures and assigned readings of the first. So, if a fledgling doc hadn't quite settled into the whole academic scene during what amounted to first semester–it didn't matter much. Everyone, from the most studious to the least academically suited in attendance was on track for the same do-over presented as the second semester coursework.

The basic discourses considered imperative to setting up for the treating of ailments were:

1. Anatomy and Physiology as a single class.
2. Pathology–a fairly new theory concerning germs and things wiggling under microscopes.
3. Therapeutic Pharmacy and Chemical and Medical Jurisprudence (the ethics of "do I really need to prescribe this drug/ compound?").
4. Theory and Practice of Surgery (how everything should be located and functioning, where to cut to get to it, and how to close up afterward).
5. Materia Medica (the whole of what was known about any

substance used in the treatment or management of illness–from leg braces to smelling salts).

6.   Obstetrics was presented for the specialized treatment of diseases afflicting Women and Children.

In their second year of study, students revisited the same core subjects in more depth. Again, following the pattern of sessions one and two being identical in content. Perhaps this was modeled after the "rote" method of learning so popular in other fields of study–like the alphabet, or multiplication tables.

Even in the sciences portion of coursework there was little opportunity for hands-on work with patients. Lab work, especially in the small private institutions, could consist of students copying drawings from a large chart or chalkboard presentation. The students were responsible for their own sketches which they made during lectures. Textbooks were scarce. The material presented and beneficial to copy from the wall, ranged from anatomy to pathogens one might someday glimpse under a microscope–if they ever got to own one.

As an alternative to programs offered by traditional universities, independent proprietary medical schools were opening everywhere. Often headed by a co-op of practicing physicians, these schools were opened as a sideline to make money. Commonly, they were single room lecture halls on second floors over dry goods or feed stores in the downtown district of mid-sized towns and cities. This made the third floor available to rent to students as their living quarters. The business model of running a medical school was quite attractive to those who already owned a storefront business in their own building with a couple of floors of space overhead for rent.

In fairness, modern medicine was in its infancy. Joseph Lister, the father of sterilized instruments, didn't start cleaning surgical implements with carbolic acid between patients until 1870. And many people–both doctors and their patients–were still subscribing to the theory of disease being based on an imbalance of the "Humors."

Humors were believed to be a reflection of the elements of our world–earth, air, fire and water. The name for this theory was "Humorism" and it was the "way" of cause and effect, illness and treatment, from the time of the Greeks until late into the 1800s. One's Humors needed to be kept balanced in order for a person to be well. According to Humorism, black and yellow bile, phlegm, and blood were the go-to sources for investigating and prescribing cures against ailments.

―――――――――

As proof of a student's two years worth of classroom theory, a fancy engraved diploma was awarded to those with non-delinquent accounts.

Beware of Ghouls, Body Snatchers, Resurrectionists, and Grave Torpedos

"Unscrupulous persons endowed with steady nerves found visits to lonely graveyards on dark and gloomy nights to be a rather easy way of 'digging up' a little extra spending money." (Ralph W Stark)

Around the time citizens of means were removing their loved ones' remains from Lebanon's old public cemetery and transferring them to the (literal) greener pastures offered at Rodefer's, some unauthorized exhumations were underway as well.

Upon Rodefer Cemetery's opening in 1872, big changes were happening in medicine and at medical schools. While in 1800 there were only four medical schools in the United States, by 1872, over six dozen were open and running. Students were now paying big money to attend. The competition to increase enrollment was stiff, and schools felt the pressure. To command the highest possible fees meant that programs needed to be more scientific with practical experience–not mere theories preached from a lectern.

Specimens–human specimens–were in demand. Prisoners, those residing at Insane Asylums, and bodies of persons who died unclaimed in almshouses were all allowed and available. Unfortunately, the fair-game population wasn't dying in sufficient numbers to keep pace with demand.

The events of the Lincoln family's trials of 1865 were still fresh enough in everyone's mind. The body of our assassinated president had been targeted for theft and ransom repeatedly. Grabbing and holding a Presidential corpse for a hefty payout could be quite a moneymaker if successful, but less famous people weren't worth the risk. No one in Boone County was world-famous-valuable like Honest Abe.

Desperate medical schools didn't care about fame. They needed bodies; fresh, good quality, human bodies. So, turning a blind eye to source, they offered up cash–no questions asked. A specimen in fine shape could fetch more money than most law abiding folks earned in six months.

The lure of cash created intense competition among grave robbers. Partnerships and covert associations of "ghouls" were formed where techniques were shared and constantly evolving. In order to be first in line at the money-shoveling back door of a medical school, body snatchers needed to be more innovative, efficient, and clever than their competitors.

With the rush to turn open graves for both old and new interments at Rodefer's, people were nervous. No one was really keeping track of which piles of fresh dirt were legitimate, and which had been unlawfully tampered with. Folks were especially worried with the location of the new "digs" being situated so close to the railway–making for a fast and easy get-away.

In 1878, the smoldering embers of many folk's darkest fears were fanned.

Congressman John Scott Harrison, Hoosier-born son of our 9th President William Henry Harrison, fell victim to body snatchers.

John Scott was born in Vincennes while his father William Henry was serving as Governor of the Indiana Territory. Ironically, as a young man, John Scott went to medical school at the University of Pennsylvania (one of the original four) but disliked the field. He returned home to seek his fortune as a farmer. The Harrison family held a large stake near Cincinnati at the town of North Bend bordering the Ohio River.

Soon, politics caught the well-to-do farmer's interest. In 1852, John Scott was elected to Congress and served two terms representing the people of Ohio. Failing to be elected a 3rd time, he returned to his farm at North Bend. By this point in his life he had married twice and had fathered 13 children. Child number five, second to be born during his second marriage, grew up to be US President Benjamin Harrison.

In 1878, only days before 73 year old John Scott Harrison died, a close friend and distant relative of the Harrison family, 24 year old Samuel Augustus Devin died. The young man had suffered an accidental injury four years previous, and was also ravaged by the effects of a long struggle against Tuberculosis. Many reported that poor Augustus was no more than a "walking skeleton" at the time of his death.

To a community already mourning the loss of long-suffering Augustus, the death of family patriarch John Scott Harrison only days later was a real blow. As dignitaries and family traveled from far and wide to attend old Harrison's funeral, two of his adult sons, Benjamin and John Scott Jr, went to the family's private burial lawn at Congress Green Cemetery to survey their father's grave site. They wanted to be assured that all was ready for services. Arriving at the cemetery, they found nearby Augustus' grave, less than one week old, disturbed. Upon further investigation their worst suspicions were confirmed–the pathetic corpse of Augustus was gone.

The two Harrison brothers immediately gave the sexton instructions for their father's grave to be reinforced against any would-be thieves. They had a brick wall installed around the vault, ordered a locking metal casket, and gave instructions for the entire thing to be weighted down with two boulders cemented over the lid of the concrete vault. The Harrisons ordered loads of sharp gravel to be mixed with the surrounding soil to make digging difficult. As one final measure of safety, they hired a local man to guard their father's tomb. The guard agreed to check the grave hourly over the next 30 days.

The morning after their father's funeral, the Harrison brothers set out for the nearby Ohio Medical College where it was rumored a large package had been delivered the night before. They hoped to find the body of Augustus and return him to the devastated folks back home.

With warrant in hand and two Sheriffs along, the Harrison party demanded entry at the Ohio Medical College. After some squabbling, they were finally let inside and spent hours searching the operatories and every other part of the facility from top to bottom.

Augustus was no where to be found. In fact, the search party could find no evidence of stashed bodies anywhere.

The only corpses they saw were rankly decomposed and too fully dissected to be new. None of the tabled cadavers were emaciated; clearly, none of these could be Augustus Devin.

Feeling defeated, the group stood in the tower room discussing their next step. This upper room had been their last chance to find the remains of Augustus and return home in triumph. It was then that one of the searchers noticed the disinterested janitor tasked with escorting them room-to-room for the search, was starting to act impatient. Clearly, the employee was anxious to move the party on their way.

As the Harrisons and those accompanying them began to

shuffle toward the narrow stairway, a bit of rope was noticed on a floor board near the room's outside wall. Upon examination, a trap door was discovered covering a long dark shaft. A tug on the rope revealed that it was tethered by something heavy. They pushed the antsy janitor aside and began pulling. The men hoisted the rope several feet before making a devastating discovery. Dangling from the end of the long rope, was the hooded but otherwise naked body of a man. He was hanging by shackled ankles. They had raised the body to the uppermost floor of the tower all the way from a hidden pit behind the cellar wall.

The long body was not Augustus. This man was much older and taller. He was not skin and bones like their friend. Unhooding the corpse and turning it face-up, the onlookers were horrified to see the face of John Scott Harrison. The body they'd found was one they all assumed had been securely interred at Congress Green Cemetery. The sons wept, seeing that even the extreme precautions they'd taken were ineffective in protecting their own father.

Two weeks later, in mid June, Augustus Devin was identified as one of several bodies floating in a vat of brine in the University of Michigan's medical school basement. He was taken from Ann Arbor and brought back home to North Bend.

Newspapers across the world picked up the story. Those who made a living robbing graves were referred to as ghouls, body-snatchers or resurrectionists. No one felt their loved ones could be safe. Large cemeteries, especially those with upper-crust burials hoping to attract more of the same, ran advertisements. They bragged of night watchmen and armed patrols –brave enough to ward off any "ghoul" with a "shoot first, question later" motto.

In the wake of all these odd circumstances coming together, it is no surprise that another enterprise was spawned out of need. A former circuit court judge, Thomas K Howell of Circleville, Ohio, perfected and patented a "Grave Torpedo." The mechanical device was fixed over the lid of a coffin. If disturbed, a spring would detonate an explosive. The deceased would continue being deceased, and the would-be body-snatching-robber-ghoul, would be blown to Kingdom-Come. Howell became wealthy from his device first patented in 1878. He added an updated version in 1881 which also enjoyed great success.

It's rumored that more than one of these Howell detonators lies below the grass at Oak Hill. One is supposedly planted at the burial place of a pioneer saloon keeper's daughter. Given that there was an authorized Howell dealer in Lebanon, there may be many more. Of course, for the safety of all, the exact locations are a well guarded secret.

No one should ever go poking around to tempt fate or test the reliability of Mr Howell's patented Grave Torpedo. He felt so assured of the efficacy of his protective invention, he ran advertisements in newspapers and circulars of the day proclaiming quite eloquently:

"sleep well sweet angel, let no fears of ghouls disturb thy rest, for above thy shrouded form lies a torpedo, ready to make minced meat of anyone who attempts to convey you to the pickling vat."

A couple of years after their release, grave torpedoes were banned in most areas. Too many cemetery employees were getting injured while innocently opening new graves. The Howell devices were indeed well made; the slightest disturbance around them would cause them to detonate.

*

During 1858 in another case of body-snatching dubbed the "Celebrated Fayette Resurrection Cases" two country doctors along with two other men digging for corpses near Fayette were accused of grave robbery. Before charges could be filed for the thefts of Miss Maria Smith and Mrs Martin Shirley's remains from Smith's Cemetery, one of the young men and one local doctor fled the country. The remaining two men (one a resident of Fayette) were both tried but not convicted by a court at Crawfordsville; evidence against them was ruled too thin.

This judicial outcome was shocking, even with the change of

venue to another county. Especially because the man from Fayette confessed to having taken the bodies with the aid of two others. He further stated that the fourth man was present during the dissections.

*

In 1887 St Joachim's Catholic Church (now St Joseph) began moving their longtime cemetery from the countryside to a five acre property adjoining Rodefer's to be closer to the church. Since its founding, St Joachim had maintained a graveyard just south of the current 4H fairgrounds on a sloping hillside.

A terrible discovery was made after several months of digging up and reburying the Church's own faithful departed. In June of 1887, *The Lebanon Pioneer* reported that the body of John Sullivan was missing from his grave. Sullivan had been a physically large, powerful man. Being a fine specimen in life, Sullivan's body would have fetched a handsome price as a cadaver. He'd died more than five years before the Church began closing and moving the location of its cemetery. With so much time having passed between the crime and the discovery, there was nothing to be done.

*

As late as 1902, bodies were still being snatched by ghouls. Former resident, Rosa Neidlinger was living just across the Boone-Marion line when she died at age 22 of consumption (tuberculosis). She was laid to rest at Pleasant Hill Cemetery between New Augusta and Trader's Point. Two months after burying his wife, bereaved husband Manson Neidlinger received a phone call from a stranger telling him an unthinkable story. The unknown caller told Neidlinger that if he went to Pleasant Hill and opened the grave of his beloved Rosa, he would find it empty. However, if he wasted no time, he had a chance to reclaim her body from Central College for Physicians and Surgeons at Indianapolis (forerunner of the Indiana University Medical School).

If recovered, the mystery caller demanded to be compensated

for assisting Neidlinger by providing this information. Adamant he would agree to no such deal, Rosa's husband enlisted the help of his friend and New Augusta Constable, James Cropper in his search (relative of Zionsville's longtime furniture builder and undertaker, E S Cropper). When the men arrived at Rosa's grave it appeared completely undisturbed. Manson's friends urged him to drop the whole thing and to take the telephone call as a terribly sick joke. Rosa's husband insisted he would not leave until he saw his beloved Rosa still inside of her coffin with his own eyes.

After a long while digging, the lid was in sight. The men raised the top of the coffin and found it to be empty. Wasting no time they went directly to Indianapolis and obtained a search warrant from Prosecutor Collins and an escort by two bicycle patrol officers. When they were refused admittance at the gated entrance, Neidlinger's party sought the assistance of more local police.

Going back with reinforcements, the men were allowed inside. They were given a tour of the disecting room but only found one table bearing the body of a woman. At last a barrel was spotted and ordered opened for inspection. Reluctantly the interns pried off the top and Neidlinger immediately recognized the corpse of his wife.

Eventually the large organized band of men responsible for the grave robbery of Rosa Neidlinger were all captured and convicted. The caller was never identified, but was suspected to be a member of a rival ring of ghoulish resurrectionists; trying to profit from another thief's success.

Boone Stuff Worth Knowing

⸾⧓⸾

"Ten cents per line will be charged to all businessmen who did not advertise while living. Delinquent subscribers will be charged fifteen cents per line for an obituary notice." (notice from The Lebanon Patriot, August 1895)

*

James Whitcomb Riley was a Boone County poser. In 1882 he was often writing under the pseudonym "Benj F Johnson of Boone County." One of his most beloved poems was published under this pen name by *The Indianapolis Journal* on June 17th of that year–*The Old Swimmin-Hole*. During the 1880s and 1890s Riley made many visits to our county. He was a popular and frequent orator at the Grand Opera House in Lebanon.

*

If you talked in church, you were going to get a good sharp pinch. But if you didn't heed the pinch and "acted up" anyway, then at a time when you were all alone and least suspected it–the earth would open wide, swallow you up and you'd never be seen again. That's how kids disappeared.

*

As everyone could tell you long before weather radar, rain is to be expected when cows lay down in the fields. The barometer change makes their milk supply feel extra heavy and that tends to give them a backache.

*

The closer the rain gets to you, the more the leaves on maple trees will curl up and turn inside-out.

*

Skies suddenly tinged bright yellow (even during the mildest rainstorm) could turn an other-worldly shade of green in a heartbeat. Those kind of eerie-looking skies were your cue to gather the photo albums and kids. You would all then stand vigil before the house's largest window on the lookout for approaching tornadoes.

*

In case of Tornado-looking weather, everyone was advised to seek shelter after performing the following civic-bound duties:

1. Call local law enforcement to report suspicious cloud formations or confirmed touchdowns
2. Open at least a couple of windows to prevent the building you were sheltered in from "imploding."
3. Consult your black and white television set for atmospheric signal disturbances caused by an approaching twister (via a very detailed list of formulaic tasks called the "Weller Method," first touted in the 1960s) .
4. In homes with basements, once a tornado was spotted, your best bet was to seek shelter in the corner nearest the expected point of impact.
5. If you were living without underground shelter, you'd be forced to ride-it-out in a bathtub while holding a mattress over everyone's head.
6. Nobody with a bit of sense ventured away from their shelter before all the shaking, roaring and thumping turned to dead silence.

7. If caught out in the open, the best advice was to immediately run away from the funnel's path at a right angle while loudly confessing all the sins you'd ever committed.

*

If you were in need of a new well, you'd best call up a Witch; though some of them preferred to be called a Diviner or a Douser. These weren't Halloween witches, these were men graced with the gift of being able to locate a good reliable water source by use of a willow branch and their mind. A good one could witch a well that would run clean and wet for a man's entire lifetime.

*

Before soil testing was widely available (and accepted as science rather than voodoo) crop farmers tested their own soil before planting. This helped them to know what to plant and if any amendments were needed (like running the hogs down to the field for some "fertilizing" a few weeks before tilling). This was an art or gift just like locating a good well. And frankly, men who didn't have this skill, rarely found success with crops. They might be able to raise livestock, but a family could lose everything pretty fast if a year's crop wasn't chosen accurately.

*

A farmer who knew his stuff walked out into the middle of each of his fields as soon as winter broke. He'd grab up a fist full of earth, and squeeze it hard. The behavior of the compressed dirt was noted as the farmer went on to the next test. Holding the same soil in one hand, he would bust up the clod he'd just made, releasing a sample of the field's aroma. Smelling the dirt for a few minutes added more clues to its condition.

*

For some farmers, this was enough information. Other fellows went the extra mile and actually tasted the sample as

another measure of judging the ground's needs for the coming
season.

*

Everyone knew a corn crop that didn't reach the standard
"knee high by the 4th of July" would fail.

*

As a "young buck," my Grandpa George like many fellows of
his generation, dug graves for extra cash. Using a garden shovel
and a pickax, each grave opened earned diggers $2.50. "Back then"
he used to boast, "that was enough for me and my girl to go to
dinner and the show."

*

Sticking out your tongue at somebody, or even scowling at a
plate loaded with lima beans alerted any nearby adult to warn
you "Straighten up! What would you do if your face froze like
that?"

*

A kid could anticipate their own death upon hearing Mom
speak the words "Just wait until we get to the car!" Worse yet, a
double death (one suffered by the anticipation alone) was in store
when threatened with "Go to your room and wait for your Father
to get home!"

*

Another tried and true psychological torture aimed at kids
was the old "Well, you've done it now! Just march out into the
yard and cut me a switch!" This meant you were about to get a
whoopin. But it was also a way to throw a kid into the swirling
vortex of real conundrum. The thin flexible branches (switches)
of a young sapling stung like a whip–they were *the worst*! But if a
kid tried to navigate around the thin whippy ones and go for a
stiffer, sturdier stick to pass off as a switch, parents were wise to
the ploy and would compensate by delivering more swats. Pretty
much, the "go cut your own switch" level of trouble was a no-
win; sure to end with days of sitting gingerly.

*

Never make an adult "stop this car."

*

Do not stand behind a horse

*

An invitation to dinner is an invite to a noon-time meal.
Supper is served after five.

*

Drinking a beer (for some long forgotten reason) on Sylvia
Liken's grave is a Boone County right of passage.

*

People are not fat. They are husky, big-boned or sturdy.

*

Homemaker's Clubs are ways for Moms to stay in 4H forever.

*

Holiday Road is almost as scary as Lost Road, but nothing is
scarier than the House of the Floating Candle.

*

No place ever made better tasting food than what was served
every year at the old Bee Hive during the 4H fair.

*

If you were ever arrested, everyone read about it in the next
day's newspaper. Especially if a stay at "Club 104" was involved,
or it had anything to do with the famed "1935 Beverage Act"

*

If you were dare-devil enough to go tearing down a gravel
road with your windows rolled down, you'd better not slow up.
Otherwise, be prepared to eat dirt, wipe it out of your eyes, ears,
and every other nook and cranny of your body for days. Your car
would never again be safe for wearing white clothes, and you'd be
destined to have dirt-brown boogers for a week.

*

Truly
There Is No Place Like Boone

*

Photo of a turn of the century establishment, serving fancy drinks and a variety of cigars.

From the Ralph W Stark Heritage Center at the Lebanon Library–Image Collection

Immoral Boozey Boone

⸙

"The foundation for a brick saloon was begun last Thursday at Thorntown to the utter disgust and bitter mortification of a number of citizens." (from The Lebanon Patriot, 1884)

Before Prohibition, the south edge of Lebanon's square was bordered by a long string of one bustling saloon on top of another. Locals referred to the area as Skid Row or the Bowery. The bars, breweries, gin mills and taverns tried uplifting their image by rebranding themselves for a while as "tasting rooms." The city's 1887 business directory listed a cluster of 10 tasting rooms at side-by-side addresses.

A referendum vote taken around this same time showed the community squarely split on the topic of temperance. With approximately 1300 votes cast, the margin of victory in favor of saloon operation was less than 50 votes. Booze was a divisive topic across the county and within the whole state for years.

Adding to the public nuisance of drunken saloon patrons was a flourishing trade in prostitution. One bawdy-house run by a "Madam H" on Lebanon Street was particularly loathed. Situated away from the area of the Bowery and its general debauchery, the brothel was in an otherwise "nice" neighborhood. The scandalous house was a blight on the area for years. In 1890 the enterprising tenants were finally ousted by the landlord who buckled under pressure from angry women's groups and temperance leagues.

Even without Madam H, the Lebanon prostitution problem persisted. It continued lustily, existing hand-in-glove with the saloons of the old south side. Newspaper reports often announced that all brothels doing business in the rooms above bars of the Bowery district had been cleared-out once and for all. A few days later, the same paper might report that several ladies of the evening were selling dalliances at the old cemetery.

On many occasions, citizens opposed to the immoral trades took matters into their own hands. In separate incidents, a gin mill in Lebanon was blown up, a brothel was wildly attacked with sledge hammers (destroying the place down to the wall studs) and a saloon in Thorntown was bombed.

The "rough" section of our sizable county seat consisted of a few blocks known as the Evans Additions. Locals called the area Evansville. The housing tracts were bordered on the south by Noble Street, and to the east by Evans Street. The additions terminated on the north where the neighborhood abutted the train tracks running into the Big Four station near downtown. Their west edge backed up to a scrubby wooded area where townsfolk dumped dead animals and other rubbish.

Shootings and fist fights, drunken pranks and antics involving rock throwing and arson were all common occurrences in Evansville. With such a history, it really is a wonder that any of those homes could still be standing today!

If you have an 1870s-era house in that part of Lebanon, take a look at the abstract or deed of your home to see if it was built as a part of an Evans Addition– what was once considered Evansville–the "wild side" of Lebanon.

Even Whitestown, a much smaller town, was not immune to the ills afflicting its big-city neighbor Lebanon. In the late 1880s, a newspaper article called Whitestown "a cursed place, filled with gambling dens and card halls."

When Prohibition was Constitutionally mandated in 1920, anti-dry people across the country found other ways to drink. The people of Boone County had been prepared by years of an on-again-off-again status as a dry county. For those who were wealthy enough, there were speakeasies and private clubs. Others found medicinally labeled alcohol at the corner pharmacy. Those with the least cash to spare either made their own spirits, or turned to local bootleggers.

Some unscrupulous sellers passed off watered-down wood alcohol as potable grain alcohol. Wood (methyl) alcohol was used as an industrial cleaning agent. Bottles of "cleaning fluid" were sometimes elaborately decorative and deceptive looking–implying with a wink that the real contents were actually consumable.

The notorious Colombia Spirits Company sold fancy labeled bottles filled with a deodorized version of wood alcohol. They avoided penalties by frequently changing names and denying that their product was a "wolf in sheep's clothing." In its natural state, methyl reeks of an ammonia-like fume. No one would ever want to drink the vile stuff, so it was often mixed into something else to offset the taste and smell.

Through a process patented in 1890 to make industrial use less offensive to workers, the noxious odor was removed. That's when deodorized methyl came to market. Even for its intended use, the odorless product was still dangerous. Many deaths were attributed to the use of the less offensive smelling solvent by workers forced to use it in areas without sufficient ventilation.

In 1911, a drinking party with eight in attendance at Whitestown resulted in one man being permanently blinded and four others laying dead within 48 hours. The culprit was alcohol poisoning. Both the town and Dr PB Little became quite famous from the event.

Dr Little was quoted and interviewed many times over the next ten years about his study of the *Whitestown Alcohol Poisonings*. It was purely by coincidence that Little was an area physician as well as one who subscribed to an newly popular (and much touted by Sigmund Freud) theory concerning vapors and glandular health.

Although he did not personally treat any of the afflicted, Dr Little wrote of the poisonings in this report which he shared to the Indiana State Board of Health and other entities:

"It seems that these men purchased and made a mixture of 1 gallon of wood alcohol and 3 gallons of grain alcohol and all drank freely of it. The symptoms that followed soon after were chiefly headache, nausea, vomiting, extreme weakness, clammy sweats, weak pulse, blindness, dilated pupils, cyanosis, sighing respiration, convulsions and death. The blindness came on six to eight hours before death. The survivor of this debauch was the first to fall sick and the first to go blind."

Frank James was the man Dr Little mentioned as first to fall ill and then go blind. James had always boasted of being a close cousin to Missouri outlaw Jesse James. Folks in town didn't believe a word of his claim. James, being a known bootlegger, was not well thought of by many. Some claimed that he was a cheat, being in the habit of adding wood alcohol to his own homemade product to "give it more kick."

The bad booze was consumed on a Tuesday evening. The eight men passing the jug around that night in Whitestown were known toppers (heavy drinkers).

Frank James awoke sick and blind the next morning. Others started dying a few hours later.

Robert Hoop and his father William were with James Tuesday night. Robert not only had a reputation as a topper, but also as a hopeless consumptive. When he suddenly died Wednesday afternoon, no one connected the cause to what he'd been doing the night before.

While sitting with the dead body (as was customary at the time) Robert's father William Hoop was drowning in grief and feeling sleepier by the minute. As he and friends awaited the local undertaker, old William drank from a bottle of spirits. Others who witnessed the event said that shortly after the embalmer left, the elderly Hoop was stricken blind.

Before midnight, William Hoop was dead; laid out next to his son.

Ira Neese was one of the witnesses to William's death. He and Julius Dobson consumed some of the deadly concoction along with Frank James and the Hoops the night before. In reverence and sorrow, Neese and Dobson sat up all night at the Hoops' home watching over both of their dead drinking pals. They found William's bottle and shared it between them. In the morning, Ira went to his job at the town barbershop as usual. He only shaved one customer before declaring himself too worn out to work more without resting. Dead tired from the long night, Ira Neese went home to take a nap.

Neese never came back to the barber shop that afternoon. At closing time his boss stopped by to check on him. He found Ira Neese in his home convulsing on the floor and complaining of unbearable pain. His sight was already gone. A doctor was called who diagnosed his symptoms consistent with poisoning by arsenic. Nothing could be done. Neese died soon after the doctor arrived.

Thursday evening, Julius Dobson's family sent for their own family doctor. Julius was the youngest of the party-goers. Like the others, he'd completely lost all vision and had fallen into a deep sleep. By then, word was getting around of a mystery illness overtaking the town.

Although the doctor was able to rouse Dobson enough that he woke briefly, the young man could do no more than open his eyes. He uttered nothing before suffering a single episode of convulsions and expiring.

William Lowe and Harve Sarter also attended the deadly drinking party. Fortunately for them, they didn't consume much before calling it a night. They both became ill, but recovered without any long term effects. Moses Proffitt partook as well, but disliked the taste and left after one sip. He was fortunate to survive completely unaffected.

No one knew what was really happening until four men had already died. Completely blinded, and so ill that recovery was doubtful, Frank James was probably terrified. The bootlegger started talking. He confessed to hosting the party and also to adding a little dab of methyl into the jug as a "kicker."

James claimed he had purchased the wood alcohol in an unmarked bottle from Louis Haag's pharmacy in Indianapolis on Illinois Street (later to become the large Haag's drugstore chain). But after a lengthy investigation, neither Louis Haag, nor his store was charged with wrongdoing.

Generously, none of the deceased men's families asked for Frank James to be arrested or held liable. All felt that his permanent disability was punishment enough.

Though long estranged, Frank James' married daughter took pity on him. She moved her father from Whitestown into her home south of Zionsville where she cared for him through his old age.

No record was found telling whether Frank James ever gave up drinking.

Swampdoodle was Real

I wish I could show you the little village where I was born. It's so lovely there...I used to think it too small to spend a life in, but now I'm not so sure." (Mary Kelly)

In researching the State of Boone both far and wide, I had the eye-opening experience of discovering many of the villages, bergs, towns and settlements lost to time. Yes, Swampdoodle, was only one of many.

Some of the names seemed to be made up by hecklers. Maybe they were lighthearted scraps of adoration; like when a big brother nicknames his little sister Monkey Face or Twin Piggies, and it sort of sticks for life.

Here's a listing of the town names (and I do use the term town loosely) once a part of everyday conversation. Instead of giving a long winded coordinate-type street address, you could just say you lived "out by the Old Berg" and everyone knew generally where to find you.

Many places had a revolving door on names. Some were named once and it stuck. A few, like Jamestown, have residents who seem bent on confusing non-locals by calling the place both Jimtown and Jamestown in the midst of the same conversation.

Challenge yourself, family and friends. Ask them if they've ever driven through Royalton or Thornley (and knew it!).

How many of these places can you locate or relate to? Some were abandoned long ago. Some still appear on maps; even though there may only be a single building standing where a community once thrived. Geographically a few shared the same spot, but were renamed (some several times). Maybe you live in the suburbs of a little hamlet you never knew existed. Give it a try, and be sure to let me know if you find any I missed!

Lebanon, Fayette, Thorntown, Zionsville, Northfield, New Brunswick, Mechanicsberg, Hamilton, Whitestown, Milledgeville, Jamestown, Royalton, Elizaville, Max, Lickskelute, Heistandville, Advance, Rodmans, Ratsburg, Maple Grove, Spicklepoint, Gadsden, Gumble Corner, Clearfork, Gadsdell, Rosston, Northfield, Dulith, Eagletown, Reese Mills, Mt Zion, Gladsville, Hoosierville, Adamsville, Swabtown, Pisgah, Idylwilde, Locust Grove, Quiet Corners, Poverty Hollow, By-the-Way, Adams Corner, Hingers Corner, Georgetown, Jacksons Run. Dry Branch, Owl Roost, Loafers Corner, Sorghum, Whipporwill Valley, Browns Wonder, Beech Grove, Walnut Grove, Swampdoodle, Buzzards Roost, Dot, Center, Little Chicago, Possum Trot, Terhune, Kimberlin, Crackaway, Pike, Scarce, Cason, Frogs Glory, Lizzards Run, Dover, Pikes Crossing, Stringtown, Bakers Corner, Sugar Plain, Big Springs, Waugh, Ward, New Germantown, Fairview, Shepherdsville, Dillard, Herr Station, Cutts Grove, Ottinger Corner, Yubedam, John Robinson Woods, High Bluff, Morrison Hill, Herdrichsburg, New Burg, Old Burg, The Burg, Englewood, Northern Depot, Woodbine, Thornleyville, Holmes Station, Irishmans Run, Slabtown, and Evansville

A big thank you to Mr and Mrs John Armand Glendenning for loaning me their very old (c1870) photo of a fab-four set of brothers. The numbers next to their faces represent seniority and pecking order in the family. These guys inhabited the town of Shepherdsville–now abbreviated to Shepherd on many maps. There isn't a single trace of it left. The Glendenning brothers had a general merchandise store there and a post office. A fine barbershop and a blacksmith once did business at Shepherdsville as well. Nearby was a schoolhouse. Just to the south of the village was another dot on the map touching Shepherdsville Road, Herr. Herr Station was never a town and didn't have a post office. But with it's grain elevator next to the rail road tracks, it earned a name as a train stop and local destination. Pioneer decedent Ben Herr, who donated the family cabin and moved it to Lebanon's Memorial Park, lived in this small corner of Boone County.

Old Time Schools
of Boone

∞

In 1910, when school consolidation started, there were approximately 9300 schoolhouses in Indiana, about 123 of which were in Boone County. (from the historic Howard School website)

Education in the State of Boone started in homes. As neighborhoods formed, schools were set up in one-room, low ceiling structures made from chinked logs. Families pooled their resources to hire teachers; splitting the salary and expenses among those with students. Known as "subscription schools," none of them were publicly funded. Some shared space with churches and other semi-public buildings. Boone County pioneer children were educated in the same ways described in the stories of Abe Lincoln's youth. Occasionally called *Blab Schools*, all students from first through eighth grade were taught together as a whole.

Around the turn of the 20th century, county-funded and built schools were erected. Still using the open, one-room format, they were considered modern and improved being of masonry construction. Remnants of several one-room brick school houses are scattered across the county. Some have survived because they were converted into private homes or kept in good repair as farm outbuildings.

Perry township Schoolhouse #1, was brick, and considered an improved school. Also named Howard School, it has been fortunate to fare the test of time better than most over the years. The school was in use from 1881 until 1916. Sitting in the area formerly known as White Lick, the old building was gifted to the community by the Washburn siblings and taken under the wing of area residents in 2004. Through tireless hours, the group gathered grants and community support to restore the school, its grounds and the adjoining graveyard. Before the work began, the long neglected property used for farm storage was overgrown and partially roofless. The building was in generally frail condition and heavily vandalized.

Now Howard's is available as a living history museum for school children and other groups to tour by arrangement. The graveyard at the east edge of the yard is also cataloged and kept well manicured. It is an amazing glimpse into our ancestor's early years both as pupils and school masters.

Naming schools in a dignified manner was not a priority to early citizens. Some of the oldest names seem intent on poking fun at learning. They were given comical names like Corn Bread College and Hardscrabble. Another common practice was for subscription schools to be named after the schoolmaster in charge. Thus, names changed when a new master or marm was hired. At times, naming honors went to the family who donated the land where the school stood.

A few were sponsored by church congregations or township groups (though not the township government) and thus their neutral name reflected that underwriting. Later, as public funded school systems came into being, buildings were renamed by their township and assigned a number (like Howard School's other name–Perry #1).

Here is a list of schools that once existed in Boone County, accounted for by name, not by number. See if you are able to identify one nearby that hasn't seen a pupil or a sign post in years. Even if you look for none of them, some of the names may raise your eyebrows. You also may discover a branch of your own family tree was responsible in some way for educating young Boone citizens.

Big Springs, White School, Nicely School, Dover, Wells, Dutchman, Wentz, Mts Run, Northfield, Hill School, Hazel College, Englewood Consolidated, Cynthian, Dillard, Faulkner, Lumpkin, Buncomb, Poplar College, Perry Township Common, Baker's Corner, Bell School, Sugar Plain, Taylor, Fountain School, Union Township, New Jamestown, Old Center Ridge, Thorntown Academy, Mudlick, Presbyterian Academy, Swamp College, Royalton, Pitzer, Goodnight, Crossroads, Fountain School, Thompson School, Terhune District, Smith School, Tamarac, Crabapple, Millidgeville, Ratsburg, Parr, Bellas, Hopewell, Elizaville, Howard, Beck School, Cory School, Northfield, Hazel College, Max, Stokes, Southside, Harney, Northside, Bear Slide, Mud Creek, Belles, Mechanicsburg, Clinton Township, Buzzard Roost, Hardscrabble, Crawford Home, Boyer School, Center, Lindbergh, Miller School, Advance, Cherry Grove, The Colored School, Old Jaques, Granville Wells, Hazelrigg, Jamestown, Wright School, Waugh, Buntin, Lister, Frogs Glory, Hoboken, Eagle Township, Zionsville, Corn Bread College, Hazel Thicket, Vidito School, Perry Central, Heady, Bean School, Shiloh, the Lebanon Private, Eagle, Pinnell, Bert Caldwell School, Spring Creek, The Hill School, Washington Township, Bushtown, Harrison Township, Sharon School, Burns School, Lebanon High School, Yates, New Brunswick, Elm Swamp, Crane, People's College, Sleepy Hollow, and Schenck's School

---

*Note: I've spelled them as they were noted in the various sources I discovered them in.

Mary Mary Mary

"He Assaulted Mrs Mary Ackers, A Respectable White Woman–A Crowd Gathered at Lebanon"   (Indianapolis Journal February 5, 1894)

Shortly after supper Mary Akers put her children down for the night. She was 33 years old, raising five small children by two husbands; neither at her side.

In 1894 darkness crept in early and long between Christmas and Easter. A light February snow whipped its way toward earth landing in swirls on the frozen fields of Boone County. Moonlight obscured by clouds gave away hints of nothing but blackness in the wind.

The oldest four were from her first marriage. Linus Staton was a good man; a hard working farmer. There had been love and the promise of a solid future between them. Married in 1881, Linus and Mary bought a modest farm situated near their two families and set up housekeeping. Seven years into their union, Linus was stricken with Typhoid fever. A fighter at heart, he suffered for 21 days before succumbing. His tragic end left Mary alone with three small children–newly pregnant with a fourth.

After Linus' passing, Mary worked hard. She swallowed her pride for the sake of the children and accepted the help of her nearby parents, siblings and in-laws. The whole community marveled at the pretty little widow's bravery and determination. With so many helping, Mary's crop and farming receipts that year netted enough to pay off the debt of Linus' funeral.

Grateful to have that hurdle behind her, Mary started feeling stronger. She could see her way forward and hoped to make a life for her family. Looking with optimism toward the future, Mary hoped someday she would also be able to pay off the note on her farm.

In 1891 she made the acquaintance of a neighbor, John Akers. John had just moved back to Boone County after living in Wisconsin. He had lost his wife shortly after giving birth. John was left alone to raise their baby girl.

Though John Akers' infant daughter was enumerated with him during the 1880 census in Wisconsin, no record shows a child living with him upon his move back to Boone County. Had John suffered another misfortune before meeting the pretty widow-lady down the road?

For Mary's part, she may have been lonely, or felt having a man in the house would bring her some peace of mind. The widowed neighbor seemed an acceptable match. Mary also didn't like the thought of imposing on family indefinitely. She decided to welcome a man into her life again.

Mary and John Akers wed that summer. By fall, she was carrying his child.

Less than three years later, husband number two was–as folks called it back then– "out of the house." Like his infant daughter on the Wisconsin census, there was no way to trace the reason for John Akers' absence. Was he put-out by her, did he run off, or was it just a situation of mutual parting?

That February night, Mary was alone; an Akers only by virtue of her youngest child and her fairly new last name. Whatever the reason for John's absence, everyone in the community considered her to be nothing less than an upstanding and tragically unfortunate woman.

No records were found to indicate a divorce, annulment, or dissolution by abandonment. Akers was just gone. He reemerges a few years later via a marriage recorded to another woman in Crawfordsville. He lived out his days with her, dying of Stomach Cancer in 1905. He is buried without a spouse near his sister Mary Akers Bradley at Center Cemetery, Lebanon.

The nighttime silence broke abruptly with a loud rap on the door. Pulled from sleep, Mary was muddled and wondering if she'd dreamed the sound. To avoid waking the toddler who shared her bed, she struck a match and lit her lantern with a low wick.

Mary jumped when she heard the knock again.

Moving quietly out of bed she noted the hour. It was already past ten. Still foggy from sleep Mary worried what sort of emergency this could be. Her house sat a half-mile back from the road amid nothing but fields and outbuildings. Her nearest neighbor lived a full mile away.

Making her way toward the door, the rapping happened again. This time a loud voice broke through the dark silence. Fully awake now, Mary was scared.

"Miss Akers! Open up the door Miss Akers! I've got a wagon load of your friends. I taxied them out here from town Miss Akers. They're waiting for you!"

Mary cracked opened the door.

Holding up the dim lantern she recognized the man who stood before her in the darkness. She knew Frank Hall by name but little more. He was the married son of a colored family whose farm was a few miles away. Over his shoulder, there was no wagon loaded with friends.

Hall thrust his hand past the doorway. He grabbed at Mary as she let out a scream. He warned her to "keep quiet," but she kept yelling and trying to dodge his reach. Hall pulled a revolver from his coat. Mary stiffened with fear. He reached again and yanked her tight against him, Hall put the gun to her temple and threatened Mary again. By now the scuffle had roused the children who had come into the room and were crying frantically alongside their mother. Mary kept screaming and trying to fight him off.

Hall pressed the gun tighter to her head and nodded toward the bedroom door; this time adding that he'd kill the children if she uttered another sound.

Noise didn't matter. Late into a winter night, in the middle of nowhere, no one could hear the small woman's pleas for help. Hall ordered the children away from their mother's room. Huddled together in the next bedroom the children cried softly, hearing their mother being beaten and struggling on the other side of the wall. Finally, the man's heavy footsteps moved across the floor. The front door was abruptly pulled opened and then shut. They listened as Frank Hall skipped off the porch with a few quick steps.

Hall had assaulted and raped Mary for nearly an hour.

To avoid the roads while making his escape, he ran across the empty winter fields to his home two miles to the west.

Mary watched from the window as he disappeared into the darkness. Sure he was gone, she pulled on clothes and tried to console the children. Leaving her 10 year old son in charge, she urged all her children to be brave. Saddling the horse to fetch help, she promised to return for them with their uncle Isaac. She rode east into the darkness toward her brother's home three miles away.

It was almost midnight when Mary found herself sobbing with desperation while banging on Isaac Isenhour's door. On her brother's porch, the sound of her own knocking made Mary wretch. Each rap recalled the noise she had woken to. The nightmare and humiliation she had just survived was sinking in. Waiting in the cold, she banged again hoping to hurry family to her aid.

While their mother rode to uncle Isaac's for help, Mary's children cowered together in their bedroom. Hearing a man's footsteps approach, they dared not move before they heard their uncle's voice. When the man said nothing, they peered underneath the bedroom door. Together they watched with horror as Frank Hall's form reentered their home. Using Mary's still-glowing lantern, he looked around for a moment before finding the pair of gloves he'd left behind. The children remained frozen with fear, watching until Hall left their home again.

Mary's brother Isaac alerted in-laws, brothers and all the other men of the neighborhood. Even though the hour was late, he sent a pair of men for Sheriff Troutman at Lebanon. Escorted by an armed party, Mary rushed back home. She crumpled to her knees as the sobbing children told of Hall's reappearance.

Tracks impressed on the fresh snow confirmed what the children said. A few men in the party followed the prints and found that they led directly to Hall's farm. Those who stayed back, kept a close guard over the traumatized children and their mother. Mary bundled the youngsters up to protect them from the frigid darkness. The armed men rode alongside the family wagon. Together they shepherded Mary and her children along the lonely road to the safety of Isaac's home.

Discussing the matter with Sheriff Troutman, the men decided on the best course of action. A few would volunteer to watch Hall's house from a distance overnight. Isaac and his brothers would go into Lebanon before daybreak with Sheriff Troutman and wake Judge Fields. The men agreed to follow the protocol of law; nothing further would happen before a warrant was obtained for Frank Hall's arrest.

When the sun rose, all of Hall's tracks were visible. The snow had stopped falling before he took his first run across the hardened dirt. Judge Fields signed the warrant. Marshal Oden joined the party of men who rode northeast out of the city. They arrived at the Hall place around seven on Sunday. By then their party had grown to 70 men. The law abiding riders surrounded the home. Troutman and Oden served the warrant taking Hall into custody without incident.

*

When the lawmen and their posse rode back into Lebanon, they were alarmed by what they saw. A dangerous situation was brewing. Sunday morning streets were usually peaceful at the county seat. However, the news of the previous night's events had spread like wind born sparks over dry kindling. Folks from all around the county were gathered in whispering groups on the courthouse lawn. As the riders approached the jail with Hall in their custody, they felt the eyes of more than one hundred angry citizens staring in their direction. Soon, crowds coming out of Church services were lured by the unusually populated square. The whole town was abuzz–more people kept coming.

By noon, Sheriff Troutman was worried. The old jail was built to keep prisoners *in*. There wasn't much to keep an angry mob *out*. Making matters worse, the Sheriff's own living quarters were attached to the jail. Troutman's family was behind the same doors tasked with holding back the surly crowd.

For the safety of all concerned, Sheriff Troutman decided to take his prisoner into the city by train.

Frank Hall spent Sunday night at the Marion County Jail in Indianapolis; far from the angry reach of Boone County citizens. On the first train Monday morning, Hall was escorted back to Lebanon for an emergency hearing scheduled before Judge Stephen Neal of the Circuit Court at nine.

Sheriff Troutman's plan to slip Frank Hall back into town unnoticed by taking the early train didn't work. Arriving at the Big Four Depot, a rowdy crowd had already assembled and was threatening violence.

With all parties consulting, a decision was made to push back the nine o'clock arraignment hearing. Delaying until two in the afternoon seemed safer. Town officials hoped the escalating group would get cold, grow tired and head home.

The weather had no effect against the crowd. By noon there were more people in town waiting to see Hall hang. Prosecutor Patrick Dutch stood at the top of the jail steps and addressed those gathered. He tried to dissuade them from making a circus of the matter. He promised he would do all he could to bring stern and swift justice in the case. Everyone listened, but no one left.

Next, the town leaders pulled a flatbed wagon up in front of the jail steps. The crowd packed the street between the jail and the north lawn of the courthouse. Reverend HL Kindig of the Methodist Church spoke from the wagon platform, pleading for cooler heads to prevail. He was followed by Reverend JA Pollock of the Presbyterian Congregation. Then Reverend Knowlton, the popular Baptist Preacher addressed the crowd. Finally Father Hellhake spoke hoping to catch the ear of any Catholics stubbornly standing firm. Though all listened with polite attention to the four regarded clergymen, none left and more people filed into the town square.

The situation was escalating out of hand.

Mary's brothers escorted her and the children into Lebanon that morning. In turn, they each verified that the man held in the jail was the same man who had entered their home and brutalized Mary. Their accusation contrasted sharply with the story that Hall was telling.

When questioned as the warrant was served, Frank told those arresting him that he had been nearly home from Lebanon at the time Mary was attacked. He insisted he had been in his own bed before ten. At the same time in a separate room, his father Levi Hall told the warrant officers that he'd heard Frank come in around midnight.

Levi Hall was brought into the city to talk with his son. Along with Prosecutor Dutch, he persuaded Frank to plead guilty for his own immediate safety. Both men feared Hall would not survive the day–let alone a trial. Dutch solemnly promised that if Frank was indeed innocent (as he flatly insisted) he would do all in his power to see justice served. Even though he was the county's prosecutor, Dutch was widely respected as a man of his word.

As the public's behavior outside became more threatening, officials decided to secretly arraign Hall before he appeared in the courthouse.

Circuit Court Judge Stephen Neal had a full docket that day, and the melee over Hall had everyone with scheduled business at the court unnerved. For several years the structural integrity of the ornate brick courthouse had been fretted over. The foundation footings were built in the swampy soil using an assortment of locally quarried rock.

Too many of the rocks used during construction resembled bumpy clods of dirt. These were the geodes children enjoy finding near creeks and busting open with a hammer to reveal snowy crystals. Boone County's grand courthouse was built on a base akin to a bag of pretty marbles. Courthouse workers worried what might happen if a herd of several hundred angry citizens rushed the fragile building.

This was the third courthouse erected in Lebanon, and it was less than 40 years old at the time. Ironically, courthouse number three was built in 1857 to replace a two-story wooden structure that was also unsound.

Sheriff Troutman, Marshal Oden, Deputy Frank Daily and Officer James Caldwell stood before Frank Hall and opened the front doors of the jail. They were met by Prosecutor Dutch, CFS Neal (reportedly a 300 pound man built like a bull), George Norwood, WH Moler and a handful of other civic leaders who joined them to form a protective ring around Hall. An immediate uproar came from the assembly as many got their first glimpse of the accused.

Confusion and rumor spread through the crowd like a vile contagion. A woman identified by news reporters as Hattie B Taylor (some years later revealed to be Hattie Van Benthuysen) was the main agitator. She had traveled into the city that morning with a sizable length of rope. Raging and emphatically leading chants of "Let's hang him," many mistook Hattie for the woman who had suffered the assault. With a like-minded mob steadily growing around her, they pushed the hysterical woman forward. She held a pre-tied noose with both hands while the chants of "Hang him!" rallied to a battle cry.

Hattie may have been suffering from a dissociative fit of rage. One of her own young daughters had been victimized in a similar assault only weeks before at the hands of a charlatan medicine-show man. A Dr Cotton was actively being sought as a fugitive from the charges. Cotton's victim may have been Hattie's eight year old middle daughter. Records show that the Van Benthuysen family "married her off" to a young husband in another county in 1899 at the age of 13. By 1901 her obituary was in the distant town's newspaper. Hattie's new son-in-law was a widower at 21; her daughter dead from suicide at 15.

At the moment Whittaker's showy street-side clock stood precisely at two, the crowd of a few dozen boisterous and simmering individuals had swollen to more than 1000 spectators. Bracing themselves against the task ahead, Sheriff Troutman started forward.

Several attempts were made by arms coming from all directions toward Hall to stab him. Dodging penknife blades many suffered cuts as the knot of men surrounding Hall pushed forward. Troutman drew his gun in defense but in the overwhelming surge it was wrenched from his hand. Shots rang out in the crowd. Fist fights broke out along the edges of the moving scene. People farther back from the frenzied center were trying their best to hold back those bent on trouble.

The frenzied rabble (still believing her to be the assaulted widow) lifted Hattie to the fore where she successfully threw her rope over Frank Hall's neck four times. Each time the noose looped over the man's throat the crowd yanked it with such force his eyes bulged out. Three times a deputy was able to cut the line loose before Hall fell unconscious. During the fourth of the lassoing attempts, Marshal Oden was snared along with Hall. This time the rope was quickly retrieved before serious harm could be inflicted.

After several minutes of struggling against the crowd, Hall was finally behind the closed door of the courthouse.

The 70 yard march through the solid mass of citizens from the jailhouse to the north entry doors at the courthouse took them a full twenty minutes. CFS Neal used his stature to hold back the crowd. Both his physical size and his standing in the community were respected. Chants of "Hang him!" continued outside the courtroom windows. Hall was immediately brought before Neal's father, Judge Stephen Neal. No time was wasted in recording his plea of guilty. Hall was sentenced as soon as the plea was entered. He got 21 years to be served at the State Prison at Michigan City.

The outcome was announced to the boiling crowd. By then they packed the courthouse lawn, spilled out into the streets and overflowed into alleyways. A few men had climbed trees around the courthouse for a better view while yelling offers to tie the hanging rope to the limb they'd perched on. Hall was taken to Judge Neal's private chambers under guard to await the disbursement of the lynch mob. That evening, shackled and surrounded again by a ring of newly deputized, law abiding community leaders, Hall was taken to the train station to board the last run to Indianapolis. He would await transport north to State Prison while tucked away at the Marion County Jail.

Meanwhile, in a telephone call to the courthouse, an anonymous informant warned of a large well-organized protest awaiting the evening train in-hiding behind the Whitestown platform. The threat involved torches and buckets of fuel ready to set the passenger cars aflame. Though nothing materialized at Whitestown, warnings were heeded. The engineer approached Whitestown at full throttle without stopping. Hall and his escorts arrived safely at Indianapolis Monday night.

———————

Frank Hall was destined for the penitentiary. Boone County had escaped the stigma of a lawless lynching. The day that was poised to be the darkest in county history had been diffused enough that it was handled lawfully. No serious injuries had resulted.

In the aftermath of her ordeal, Mary wed again in 1895. She and husband Joe Bradley had one son and were together for 38 years. Joe died in 1933. She followed him in 1936 just shy of her 75th birthday.

On the prison intake records of Frank Hall, it was noted that he had a half brother currently serving a sentence at the same facility, and a full brother who had previously served and been released.

Frank's crime and the previous actions of his brothers must have been a terrible burden of embarrassment to their parents Emeline Derrickson and Levi Hall–but especially so to Hall's maternal grandparents.

For years, Frank Hall's Grandpa, Charley Derrickson of Thorntown, had lived in the community as a revered and beloved citizen. Charley had bought his freedom from slavery in the 1830s and then worked to buy his wife Tillie's as well. The people of Thorntown called Mr Derrickson "Uncle Charley" with great affection.

In 1900, Frank Hall was released after serving only six of his 21 years sentenced. He settled in Marion, Indiana with his wife and daughter where he went to work at Whiteley Malleable as a laborer. Within a year the couple had a second daughter. Their time together didn't last long. In 1906 Frank Hall was convicted of Burglary in Montgomery County and sentenced to another term at Michigan City.

The 1910 census finds Hall still incarcerated and his wife Leah working as a live-in cook at a rest home for the elderly in Grant county. The girls lived onsite with their mother. Leah declared herself widowed to the enumerator. Clearly Frank had used up all second chances with his wife.

———————

When I first looked into the background of this story, I saw Mary with three husbands in a very short span of time. Two of the three husbands seemed to die suddenly coinciding with a pregnancy. Red flags went up. Turning to medical journals, I began researching pregnancy-induced psychosis. Being distantly related to Mary, I worried I'd stumbled onto a genuine black widow. I also wondered if Frank Hall was somehow sucked into this twisted web as a victim. After thoroughly researching the story behind "Boone County's Near Lynching," I found quite the opposite in Mary Isenhour Staton Akers Bradley's tale. Instead of a man-killing psychopath, I found I was linked to one of the most brave and resilient women to ever live in the State of Boone.

*

In the three-day time span of these events, many reporters with vastly different opinions wrote about these happenings. They freely expressed their own bias. While several articles called the whole affair a shameful black eye to the residents of Boone County, a Crawfordsville reporter was openly disgusted by the Lebanon mob's ineptitude at "getting the job done."

*

Note: Many of the names in this story are recorded with variant spellings. I have chosen to use the one most familiar or ones I deemed through research as most likely accurate. Also, as many early settlers in Boone County were not far removed from the traditions of their European roots, several families were intermarried. For clarity's sake, I have avoided the explanations where these familial intersections happened. If you are related to the people in the story, I would be happy to share more detailed genealogies with you.

Cures that Might
Kill You

⚮

"As a remedy for flux, LH Kersey last week swallowed near two pounds of ice. It did not kill him, but gave almost immediate relief." (from The Lebanon Patriot, September, 1876)

In times closer to what may seem sensible, the folks in Boone County used certain "cures" and "receipts" against illness and daily aggravations. Many a young bride set up housekeeping with a copy of a book called *Mulierology* as a part of her belongings. The word Mulierology is kind of a made-up term to stand in for "A Woman's Role in Society, and Stuff to Help Her Survive It."

Though not attributable to a particular author, the book was some heady stuff! I am fortunate to have my own copy from 1890 securely at hand on our home bookshelf, but if you're struggling to live your life without one, you can read the whole thing via Google, free of charge.

I wonder how many young brides used the hefty volume to knock some sense into their beloveds who thought they should follow the lifestyle standards outlined in Mulierology?

Beyond the "Woman's Place" ideology offered up in Mulierology (and in countless other marital advice books of the time) a handy list of receipts for common ailments was always included. Receipt is an antiquated name for what we call "recipes." Even cookbooks were rarely without receipts for the preparation of poultices, wraps, and other cures for lame hock tendons, or sheep suffering from bloat. Kids weren't exempt from these cures. The mustard-plastered rag that improved the family mule's limp was believed to help a concussion or crush fracture on a kid's wrist just as effectively.

In the State of Boone's earliest years, cures were desperately needed. When victims of a broken bone were spared from life-threatening infection, they were often left with a useless limb or severe impairment for life. Tuberculosis was rampant and its spread was not controlled or understood. Death from typhoid fever, the ague, cholera, farming accidents, animal attack, or any form of disease now treated casually by a seven day course of antibiotics or a quick trip to Minute Clinic, could be deadly.

Childbirth was a life-or-death crap shoot too, especially when popular advice was followed to treat the traumatized birth canal and any resulting tears with a heavy packing of goose or bear grease.

Here's a short list of some of the cures that were widely touted, prescribed, and used into the late 1800s. Many were turned to again during the economic desperation brought on by two World Wars and the Great Depression. The old ways were often called upon for thrift and self sufficiency whenever cash was scarce.

Now, it goes without saying–don't try this stuff at home. Most of these potions, procedures and elixirs would get you slapped with an animal cruelty, child endangerment or possession charge nowadays. But they make for some eye-opening reading. They should also make us appreciative of ancestors tough enough to have survived not only their injuries and ailments, but to have lived through the cures as well.

- For general coughs, colds, and feverish chills–Grease the feet with a heavy coat of lard. Put to bed with stiff wool stockings

- Prepare a sugar titty for babies who are suffering colic, teething or will not sleep through the night–pack one finger of a woman's cotton glove with sugar. Tie tight with butcher string and soak the finger for a bit in good whiskey. Put the baby down to suckle on it.
- Nervous agitation, female ills or general onset of vapors may be effectively soothed by consuming tea made of a single Belladonna berry, unbruised and boiled in a large kettle of water with Valerian added as needed. The bitterness may be tempered, and the effect quickened by mixing the cure half and half with brandy.
- Afflictions of the head including aches and baldness may be treated with boiled onions, cooked to softness and then mashed and rubbed vigorously on the affected area until red. Repeat morning and night.
- When used daily to wash out the mouth, a cologne of spearmint, garden parsley and ginger root steeped together with a spoon of myrrh will keep the breath sweet.
- A thick poultice made by equal measures of strong onions and sweet turnips pounded with mustard may be applied between layers of wet cotton rags over broken bones. When swelling is abated, discontinue use of the mustard and substitute a fair amount of mugwort or wormwood.
- Dropsy (fluid around the lungs) may be improved by taking to the bed with many pillows at both head and feet and a regular dosing schedule (every three hours) with a tincture formulated from opium and foxglove. A full 30 drops must be taken at each dose; best prepared over a large spoon of sugar to diminish the mal-flavor and improve energy in the afflicted.
- Salt and honey mixed together and applied under a bandage of white willow bark, tied in place with rags or

string, will draw the sting out of bee or wasp bites, splinters, boils or other pustules.

- A piece of stale bread, the size of a nut rubbed vigorously over a wart three times daily will remove the offending bump within a fortnight.
- Broth of entrails (organ meats) from a freshly butchered calf should be fed freely to an infant with malaise and general lack of growth. This, along with heavy cream enriched with honey in place of mother's milk should spur a return to vigor.

Some do hold a bit of merit in modern medicine. Most just inebriated the patient and made them more placid and compliant for the caretaker.

The list of ways these cures are wrong (most of them deadly wrong) is probably longer than the list of cures itself!

The use of alcohol, opiates (yes, opiates) cocaine (yes–that one too) and other potentially fatal substances were common practice. These were "natural" remedies. Just as botulism is natural, or listeria or e coli is natural; natural doesn't mean it won't naturally kill you.

Instances of chemical addiction are nothing new. Many started out (just like today) as cures for painful conditions. Our ancestors were plagued by drunkenness, morphine (opiates) laudanum (opiates suspended in alcohol) and cocaine dependency (often sold in "pep-tonics" by traveling medicine shows) long before Nancy Reagan urged us all to "Just Say No."

In multiple correspondences to Generals and cabinet leaders, President Lincoln references the Soldier's Sickness (morphine addiction) as a worrisome epidemic. Men who returned home, or were still engaged in active service were injured, traumatized, and freely self medicating. He found the decline in their general health and the well-being of those around them to be dire. Lincoln recognized the urgent need for assistance and reform in pain relief. Too bad he didn't live to promote his own war on drugs.

Even the county's physicians weren't immune to the lures of self dosing with dangerous and addictive substances. In an old batch of letters and news clippings from a private collection, mention was made of a local doctor who was found dead in a roadside haystack. His death was ruled accidental. Accidental in that it was attributed to his habit of heavy drinking, followed by stiff doses of laudanum which he claimed were helpful in sobering him up in the morning. Whoa!

Indian cures were revered in the State of Boone by many. Bloodroot grew abundantly along the forest floor and was touted as a way to remove moles, cankers, cancers and worms. Black Cohosh, another common plant, was boiled and the broth was taken against joint pains and arthritis. In dried and powdered form, the Cohosh treatment was used to ease birthing pains and for menstrual cramps.

The Indian people chewed wild spearmint stems to aid digestion. They traveled with a pouch of Golden Seal for wound packing, or to chew when spirits were low. Some carried a bit of Mullein in case of diarrhea or to smoke if plagued by asthmatic spasms of the lungs.

Many Boonites refused to be treated by a white doctor if an Indian cure was available to them. It seems our ancestors were rather trendy when it came to "alternative medicine."

Don't Worry, Uncle Mose has a Madstone

One doesn't question a miracle." (Simon Beaufoy)

What I consider the wildest of the "cures" is the near-magical healing available with a "madstone." Some fortunate families left their homes in Europe securely wrapping a miracle nugget among their belongings (our ancestors from across the pond often call them bezoars). Madstones were known on the continent, especially in the Highland regions of Scotland, for centuries. Surrounded by a great deal of superstition, ritual, and mystique–one in the hands of Boone County resident Moses Nease got a lot of press coverage and was held in the highest regard.

Moses Nease (Uncle Mose, as he was called with affection) owned a portion of an exceptionally reliable madstone passed through generations of his family. This particular specimen held so much power for healing that even though it had been divided for sharing–it had lost none of its strength. With Uncle Moses' madstone on their side, folks weren't overly fearful of things like snake bites or rabies.

A madstone is somewhat like a petrified hairball from a deer. Any deer's calcified hairball will do, but the best and most powerful ones are said to be those from the gut of a white-tailed deer. Uncle Mose, the youngest of 12 children, and the father of nine, was given his piece of a Virginia white-tailed madstone by his uncle back in Cocke County Tennessee before coming to Boone County.

That Mose was gifted his portion is very important. When acquiring the powerful amulet, one may never be sold or traded. These extraordinary healing tools must only be given or found. Some have been gleaned from the forest floor. Most are discovered while cleaning the carcass of a deer felled for food and hide. If any sort of payment is exchanged over the madstone, or any cure it has caused, the stone will immediately be rendered worthless–no better than a common rock.

Some claim that a madstone can be gleaned from the carcass any cud-chewing mammal.

There are numerous stories of snake-bit livestock and persons being treated successfully with a madstone cure. But where the power to heal really stood out was in cases of people bitten by rabid (mad) animals. When treated with a madstone, the cure rate was reported to be nearly flawless–if in fact the biter had been rabid.

Perhaps the most fascinating part of this lifesaving remedy is that the stone itself knew when it could or could not be effective. When held against an animal bite, if there was venom or rabid infestation present, the stone would cling to the wound; sometimes embedding itself deep into the victim's tissue. Conversely, if the wound wasn't "mad" the stone would simply drop away.

It's said that once the hairball decided to suction itself onto a treatable injury, it became unmovable until it filled with the offending toxin; then would it spontaneously pop off. At this point it was up to the madstone's owner to quickly purify the stone (thus recharging it) and then check to see if it would reattach itself to the wound. A clean madstone wouldn't quit "pulling" until all poisons had been removed from the victim's body.

Purifying and charging the stone was a simple but important step. All that was needed was some sweet (fresh-from-the-cow) milk. Most folks either kept a cow, or had a neighbor nearby (even in town) who kept one. The stone was boiled in sweet milk before the initial application was attempted. Some stones were reported to have stuck to a wound for as long as 72 hours. When full (just like a tick) the stone dropped, signalling it was time to be boiled again.

During the purification process, poisons flowing out of the madstone caused the sweet milk to change from white to green. As toxins released out of the stone, the milk had to be changed frequently. Careful cleansing was vital. A detached stone could only be activated once fully refreshed. Severe cases might take several changes of milk to cleanse out what it had drawn up from the wound. This cycle of applying and purifying and reapplying continued until the stone refused to cling, thus signalling there was no more poison left to draw.

In emergencies where a bite happened and no milk was available, the stone could be purified with a bath of hot whiskey (which also changed color). Believers and handlers much preferred the "sanctified purity" of sweet milk when it could be had.

Mr Lewis Ullery of Lebanon discovered the value of a good madstone personally in 1886 when he was attacked by a rabid street dog. Loose dogs running in packs and were a huge problem. Called "curs" they were mentioned often in newspapers all across the county and were rightfully feared. Ullery's bite was large and open. Bystanders rushed the wounded man immediately to Mose Nease's place near Whitestown. Once the stone was applied and went through several cycles of pulling and purification, Ullery was cured.

People outside of Boone County knew and trusted the Nease madstone. Doubters only needed to meet someone who had been saved by it to become believers. Its healing was reliable and swift.

In early January of 1892, William Southard, an employee of the Kingan's Meat Packing Plant on the old west side of Indianapolis (now the site of the Indianapolis Zoo and Victory Field) was suddenly attacked by a frothing-mouthed rabid dog. Upon advice from doctors rendering emergency treatment, the man was quickly transported by train to the Whitestown depot where he was met by Moses Nease; his mad stone at-the-ready. Uncle Mose applied the cure and tended the wound for nine hours until the stone dropped and the man was fully relieved of hydrophobia (rabies). The story of the miracle healing was picked up in newspapers coast-to-coast. Reports of the incident can be found in *The Los Angeles Herald*, all the way to *The Pittsburgh Daily Headlight*.

"Uncle" Mose Nease lived from 1825 until 1910 . He is buried at Oak Hill beside his beloved wife. Most descendants have modernized the surname's spelling to "Neese." If you are acquainted with a Neese, you might want to ask them if they know whatever became of Uncle Moses' madstone–you know, just in case you ever tangle with a rabid animal or a venomous critter.

Joyriding with Freshmen on the Loop of Fear

"The State of Boone brims with the macabre, the mysterious and a full assortment of things going bump in the night." (Author and self proclaimed Terrorizer Extraordinaire–Kassie Ritman)

I suppose every community has one–a spook hill, a haunted lane, a misty, foggy, low point–where roads and legends intersect. If you're lucky, there's more than one scary place near you; places with inexplicable goings-on.

Choose in Boone from the old Indian settlements, hunting lands of ancient peoples, settlers and nomadic gypsy bands (who came to stay), hermits, eccentrics or odd men out. If these aren't scary enough, seek out the places called Lost Road, Three Sister's Bridge, the Lonely Pioneer Grave or the House of the Floating Candle.

In days gone by, it was a right of passage to experience a certain locally grown showcase of terror. Maybe it still is. The tradition was handed down to my generation from many who'd gone before us. I would imagine that these same rituals bent on scaring the pudding out of freshmen had been in practice ever since kids first got hold of cars.

All it took to qualify for your taste of terror was graduation out of 8th grade into high school. The recipe was concocted long ago; a backseat packed with witless ninth graders, plus one upperclassman at the wheel with another riding shotgun. An evening of joyriding on the loop of fear was created long ago by some uncanny local; clearly an evil genius.

I remember my own induction into the world of going to school with the big kids. As a freshman, I got my invite into a car along with a hoard of other girls after a football game. Exiting McDonald's, with milkshakes and extra ketchupy fries, we were accosted by a couple of older boys in the busy parking lot. It went something like this:

"Hey, have you girls ever seen the House of the Floating Candle?"

"No," some of us answered. A few were reluctant to acknowledge the older boy talking from the window of his mom's Buick. Others recognized him as a godlike letter-jacket-wearing Senior from our new school.

No? But you've got to see it! Come on, get in the car, we're going tonight. You won't believe your eyes!"

And so with caution thrown to the wind, car doors slamming and nervous excitement crackling in the air; off we went willingly to our doom. We had no idea what we were in-for that night: destined to be just another bunch initiated from newbies to bonafide high schoolers.

The driver was the older brother of a classmate. He was not known as a careless maniac. The sidekick's mom and was friendly with my mom, so I didn't think I would get in any trouble. What could go wrong? Especially since I was sharing the the fun with so many of my best gal-pals.

Not that it mattered to any of us whether we'd be in trouble or not–the lure was too intense–we wanted to see this curious, creepy oddity–no matter what. The upperclassmen sat in front.

We six silly freshmen were smooshed together across the luxurious bench seat–girls sitting on girls. Seat belt safety was an inconvenient hassle back then.

Imagine our excitement. We were tingling with nerves and on our way to a place known to dance between things real and impossible. We were in the car, in the moment, in the crowd. Divine! It was an honor and a thrill to be invited along on an adventure to a place that sounded otherworldly; with *Seniors* no less!

*

Three years later I earned the upperclassman status to lead these expeditions with a cohort. I admit that my friends and I lured droves of the uninitiated on our tour of the loop of terror. My reliable red Pontiac would speed up the dark highway leaving behind the safety of streetlamps swarming with creepy bats chasing June bugs. Each time we hauled a load of victims into the quiet darkness, we were armed with a head full of stories, a methodical route and several reliable stunts to get them all (male or female) screaming, crying and begging for escape.

Starting from the old Kmart parking lot, we would subtly set the mood by pointing out the bats flitting around overhead. We'd drive the innocents up highway 39 to a small road just past Sigler's diner and the Frankfort-Lebanon outdoor movie theater. If something horrible and terror-driven was flickering on the giant screen that night, all the better! Even though the images weren't visible from the road, seeing "Welcome, Now Playing: The Exorcist" on the glowing marque was enough to crack open a door to the fear of what might come next.

We'd take an old dirt road, hauling along as if demons were already within reach of the bumper. Kicking up dust and rumbling a spray of gravel from the back tires added an element of wild driving to the anticipated excitement. Zigging and zagging on twisting roads, making our way into Clinton County and then back into Boone–at last we'd come to an abrupt stop on an unkempt one-lane bridge.

The only way to find the candle we'd tell them, was by crossing this ancient, ready to crumble at any moment, haunted-remnant of a stone bridge.

Every co-conspirator who road along to the House of the Floating Candle had their own tale for the bridge. Some called it the Crying Bridge. They told a wicked tale of all the babies an old witch named Ivy swept up from cribs through open windows. She would break their necks and then toss them into the deep black eddy below. "Can you hear them?"

Oh heeby-jeebies!

Another favorite (especially when there was a good stiff wind) was the Scotland Bridge legend. This one told of the easily awakened Banshee who wailed from the underside; chained at the water's edge. He'd waited there counting as centuries passed, needing to collect enough souls to someday be released from the bridge's bondage. The Banshee was on the brink they would say, only needing another (fill in the blank with the number of car occupants) more souls to complete his unholy task.

Terror!

My all-time favorite was spun from the Three Sisters nickname for the bridge. This one got the whole car screaming every time:

There once was a wealthy farmer who owned all of the land along the Boone side of Sugar Creek. He was the proud father of three very ugly daughters. Although he had amassed huge dowries for his girls, he couldn't find a suitor for any of them within county boundaries. So, he began building a lovely stone bridge. He honored each daughter with her own perfect arch over the creek. The graceful maple trees bending over the water and road were a stunning sight to behold each fall. The new bridge made for a bucolic approach onto his valuable property.

The farmer hoped to attract young suitors from the north via the convenience of the lovely crossing. He knew once any man of ambition saw the fertile acreage, he would be further enticed by the ample dowries of his daughters. The anxious father would promise worthy suitors lifelong wealth for taking the hand of a homely daughter as his wife. However, the farmer admonished, his girls must be cherished, well treated, and closely protected so they would never suffer an unhappy moment. Else-wise, the farmer would punish the offending husband by taking all his riches away.

The bridge worked. Within a week of its opening, each daughter was engaged. The farmer was elated and planned a triple ceremony for his girls and the new sons he was about to gain. All went well. The young men took their wives and began enjoying the rewards of gentrified domestic life. Then, on the anniversary of their wedding, the three grooms took the sisters to the bridge that had ushered them into their blissful new lives. They told their hag-like brides they wanted to celebrate in the moonlight with a romantic picnic where they would present them with gifts beside a bonfire.

The homely sisters sat huddled together on picnic quilts near the fire. Instructed to "close their eyes," they anxiously awaited the opulent surprise their lovers promised if they would wait without peeking. The sly husbands wasted no time. Each savagely bashed his wife's head with a heavy bag of rocks. They then rolled the unconscious bodies into the raging bonfire. As each was assured his wife was dead, he wrapped her in the picnic blanket she'd brought expecting a romantic fireside picnic. Tying the bundles with rope, the husbands lowered their wives over the edge of the high bridge–each mockingly dangling their bride's body from the arch made especially for her. Together they lowered the burned bodies into the water. When they felt the bundles of char sink to the bottom, the men dropped the ropes, extinguished the bonfire and left. Congratulating each other, the clever husbands walked happily back to their handsome homes; each singing merrily while eating up the contents of his anniversary picnic basket.

The grooms had their farms and the money from the girls' dowries. They were rid of the ugly sisters and there was nothing the old man could do. They told him the girls had run away when they'd refused (fearing for their tender wive's safety) to take them to the Great Exposition at Chicago as an anniversary trip. In defiance, the grooms said, the sisters must have gone off together–determined to have their way and see the bright lights of the dangerous White City.

The husbands pretended to chase after their spouses, they pined falsely, they mourned with conviction, and then after a few months confessed that they had given up hope of ever seeing their dear wives again. Believing his son-in-laws, the old farmer died of grief.

But neither the farmer nor his girls ever left behind the lives and lands they were so wrongfully swindled for.

Any night when the moon is bright, you can pull up onto the triple arched Three Sisters Bridge. Turning off the car you must wait, windows down–to hear the sounds the ugly brides make as they struggle below to break through the decayed rope and swaddling layers of quilt to raise up from the mossy bed of their watery graves. Sometimes the shadow of their father appears at the foot of the bridge, walking from one side of the lane to the other–looking for the girls he can hear, but never find.

The echoing babble of water passing over rocks makes a noise that splashes and pops like something thrashing around under the bridge. Just when there is no possible way to stand another second of this horrible place the driver attempts to leave. But the car is dead. Completely unresponsive. Screams of panic escalate from the packed-in backseat occupants. With abrupt urgency, all are commanded: "Roll up your windows–lock the doors! The Farmer is coming!"

With occupants scurrying to maneuver window cranks and find doors locks the gearshift is slipped into park without notice. The driver had secretly turned off the ignition with the car still in drive.

At the last second before the farmer's shadow can grab them

from the road, like a miracle, the engine fires and merciful escape is granted.

With every successful escape, wails of gratitude spilled from the backseat.

But wait, there's more:

At this point, the visibly shaken driver would admit to feeling odd–rather lightheaded, as if they were about to slip away– lost.

"Oh my God!" the copilot would exclaim; recognizing the nefarious symptoms."We must be on Lost Road!"

"No way!–I'm sure we got away in time," the woozy driver would argue.

"Hold it together, keep driving!" the shaking voice of the copilot would command.

"There's only one way to know for sure if we're stuck on Lost Road–that's if we see the grave of the Pioneers. They got lost off the wagon train, and ended up dying here on the road. Their family dumped them into a hole and went on, to catch up with the rest of the party..." the driver's words trailed off. "What's that ahead?"

In the headlights, something small, blocky and white sits a couple of feet from the road's edge. Slowing the car–the shape takes form as a marker. Maybe it's just an old cornerstone? The driver, still feeling the effects of the bridge approaches with caution–slowing even more and aiming the high beams at the glowing slab of stone. It is small, with a patch of paving in front of it. It looks like a mistake made while building the road. At last, with the high beams perfectly angled, the dreaded words appear:

"Shepard Sr & Jr Died from Cholera 1864"

"Oh my God!" the driver and co-pilot yell in unison:

"GO, drive! WE ARE ON THE LOST ROAD–we have to get away before we're trapped here forever!"

From a standing start, the driver squeals the tires making a noise like a deranged poltergeist. Pointing the car forward while fishtailing as much as possible in the dust, the panic in the car was always palpable.

Turning right onto the first paved road, and then taking another hard right for good measure added to the authenticity. We were running for our lives. Kids went sliding around, side-to-side through the abrupt turns, screaming and crushing each other, totally out of their minds with fear.

One of the front seat elders would temporarily calm them saying: "What luck, we've escaped! Now we can get down to business. We've made it to Caldwell Road. It's time to visit the House of the Floating Candle."

By now the freshmen are dumbstruck, whimpering, or full-on crying. There is no place to turn around on this road without risking a slide-off into one of the steep ditches. *We're forced to go forward,* we'd insist. No choice at all; we were trapped until we could find a driveway. The freshmen usually settled down a bit hearing we might be turning around. Until we'd inform them—*we're only safe to travel this road with the headlights off.*

Click.

Pitch black.

I cannot imagine why no one ever jumped from a car in blind panic. Guardian angels must have joined us on every tour.

Backseat riders exchanged fear-worn glances. With feigned caution, the front seat occupants leaned forward, piloting the car slowly up the dead dark road.

A perfect thing about the country is most of the roads that look straight, really aren't. From between two cornfields at late-September height, it can look like you are engulfed on three sides at any point. Being fully surrounded by rustling leaves on stalks tall enough to hide about anything can be pretty darned scary.

The House of the Floating Candle was only approached without headlights we'd explain to them—so you could sneak past the spirits that haunted the place. They waited to catch you, grab you, and send you deep into the bowels of the hinterlands to never be seen or heard from again. The trip was risky. Some never made it back. Especially those foolish enough to approach while using their headlights or carelessly making noise.

Within seconds, the reliable pinpoint of light would be visible at the end of the road.

"Whoa! That's it–it's lit tonight!

The spirits are home! There must be a seance going on, the candle is floating!"

The back and forth banter from the front was meant to fan the fear escalating once again in the backseat.

Transfixed, the freshmen would be confused. They saw only a pinpoint of light in the distance, but kept watch in agony, trusting there would be more horribleness to come. By this point in the evening, their hearts were working double-time, trying to discharge the adrenaline spike they'd suffered less than one mile earlier.

Thankfully this road is gravel too. The rocks pinging against the oil pan add punctuation to each rider's nervous agitation. Usually by this point, the freshmen couldn't even remember *why* they were so scared, they just knew that "something" was about to get them, and that their destiny was not in their own hands.

The house–a creepy, beautifully fancied up but dark and run down brick Victorian–slowly took shape around the little point of light at the end of the road. A slightly askew gate stood a few feet in front of long-grayed porch rails. The candle stood motionless, watching from inside. No one was holding it. No shadow could be seen behind or around it–the orb of light floated midair watching our approach from behind the distorted glass of the old door. The flame seemed to quiver with excitement as the car shook the gravel. Surely the wick could see right into the soul of each one of us.

At what looked to be the road's end, the car occupants fell silent; holding their breath. Then someone in the front seat would mutter just loud enough, "I wonder if it'll follow us tonight?"

The backseat crowd thought we would be forced to turn around in the weedy dirt drive beside the gate. They were relieved when the cornfield suddenly ended on the left revealing a sharp jog in the road.

The house did not sit at a dead end as they thought, the road went around it. The freshmen were always relieved when we weren't forced to pull into that drive in order to circle back to the main road. We continued along slowly, lightless, trying to finesse our way over the rocks that moved beneath our tires. Relief would be expressed in whispered sighs and mumbles.

"Shh," the backseat wimps were warned. "Don't make any noise, we have to keep the candle from alerting the other spirits."

Creeping through the tight left turn, the candle slowed to match our speed. Leaving the window on the front door, the candle floated smoothly over to the full length window beside it; clearly watching us. If the driver sped up–the candle hopped to the next window, mirroring our pace.

With a shriek meant to startle–the driver would announce, "It knows we're here! We've been spotted!"

At the edge of the barn lot, just as it seemed we were about to get away with our lives, another sharp curve lay ahead, this time to the right. Making the change in direction in a controlled slide, we could only see the house from its west side.

From the backseat, one would reliably cry out, "It's still there! The candle is following us!"

Picking up speed for dramatic emphasis, we'd begin to fly up the dark road. The candle rushed from one window of the home to the next; chasing us relentlessly until the dust cloud and distance assured our invisibility. The freshmen would scream for mercy when the driver suddenly flipped on the headlights.

*

In no time we are back at the Kmart parking lot. The bats and June bugs they'd thought were so creepy before, seemed like friendly creatures playing tag with moths around the big bright street lamps. The underclassmen, spent with the exhaustion of what they'd just endured, untangled themselves from the backseat.

After every trip we'd roll down our windows to air out the

smell of panic induced sweat. Thankfully, there was never anything worse.

With another bunch successfully initiated, Senior partners-in-crime couldn't wait to drive to Memorial Park. We were eager to find a circle of our friends parked together en-mass to share the past hour's shenanigans with. Everyone laughed until all were gasping for air. Before long, another set of friends would pull up and share the story of their own carload's reactions that same night. None of us laughed at the kids we'd just scared as much as we laughed at ourselves; remembering our own gullibility not so long ago.

The beautiful triple-arched stone bridge was built (by the county–no farmer with ugly offspring involved) in 1901 in Clinton Township. Local contracting firm Eck & Ridout of Lebanon were hired for $4000 to build a durable bridge to cross Sugar Creek. The single lane structure was crafted completely in stone. Named Scotland Bridge, for the small town across the county line that lies a just up the road, it was placed under protection of the National Register of Historic Places in 1994. Though it is open to traffic, its best use is for the spectacular photos you can capture there–or the fun of landing one of the large carps that laze-about in the deep shady pools under the reflection of the arches.

*

Lost Road is real. Even though a green street sign has been installed to tag it by its official name "County Road 200E" most still call it Lost Road. The reason for this odd name has nothing to do with being lost from the real world on the brink of some cosmic veil. The name was given to the dirt lane in its earliest days because it crossed the creek. Conditions along the creek bank were ever changing. A sudden shower could swell Sugar Creek right up out of its banks, making a crossing impossible until the water went back down–thus the road was frequently "lost." Also, with the seasonal flooding and shifting conditions after the spring melt, the approach to the crossing varied widely. At times, mud ruts made getting close to the creek's shallow point nearly impossible. Travelers were forced to stray from the road, thus varying the route to the crossover point. The resulting mess made the crossing look as if several roads converged there. Approaching from the south to the north (or vice versa) it often appeared there were many roadways to choose. In fact, all of the little paths led back to the same single-lane corduroy road once you got far enough away from the marshy banks.

*

The roadside grave is real. The story about how it got there is not. Although quite a bit of controversy surrounds the date of events leading up to the burial–the reasoning is a tale in itself.

This is where I may get into some trouble. People do love to cling to the version of the pioneers heading west in a Conestoga wagon and dying. That inaccurate version just sounds so irresistibly distant, eerie, and tragically pioneer-ish! Even my own mom adamantly insists the urban legend is true.

The real story can be chased down via a speech given by eyewitness Mr Theodore "Dora" Caldwell, speaking in 1923 at a meeting of the Boone County Historical Society, and some official records. Although most county documents from 1856 and earlier were lost, the US Census of 1850 gives us a handy point of substantiation. Mixed into the whole mess of confusion is the errant date people see when they look at the tombstone (see my reasoning for the "wrong date" theory, with photos).

Mr Caldwell tells a story from when he was a child, living one field west of Lost Road on his family's farm. Their road, County Road 150E is still marked by its old name, Caldwell Road. Mr Caldwell begins his story around 1851, after a log home was put up and land was cleared as the homestead of neighbor, Ed Shepherd. One afternoon, Ed's father who was heading to his son's to visit, came to the Caldwell's door. The old man explained that he was suddenly feeling quite unwell, and asked if he could have assistance making the trip through the heavy brush and stand of thorn trees that separated the Caldwell place from his son's home.

Dora's father, Alexander Caldwell, dispatched his grown son Alvin to help the old gentleman make the half mile journey to Ed Shepherd's home. When Alvin returned, he reported that the man was gravely ill by the time they'd reached Ed's cabin. The Shepherd family feared the long trip had been too much for the old man, and that he might be dying. In the morning, Alexander sent his daughters Maranda and Armilda to his neighbor's home to help tend the ill father. Returning home distraught, the young women told Alexander that just as feared, old Mr Shepherd had passed. A doctor had been called, but upon arrival said it was too late for the man, and that he could do nothing for old Mr Shepherd. He diagnosed his condition as Cholera. Maranda and Armilda went on to say that their neighbor, Ed, was already beginning to show signs of the same illness.

The news of a cholera outbreak spread like wildfire through the tiny neighborhood.

Public health officials were trying to keep a gossip lid on any suspected outbreaks. News of a single case could signal an economic death pall for an entire area. Cholera was an ugly, painful death. Both it's spread and progression were rapid. The affliction seemed to settle on a population from out of nowhere and then leave just as quickly in a wake of devastation. People in nearby Mechanicsburg and Elizaville began gathering on Lost Road. They stood at the edge of the lane where Ed Shepherd's dirt drive turned off and led back 100 feet to his cabin. The panic of the onlookers was apparent as none dared to set a foot onto the path toward the home. Men and women held kerchiefs over their faces as protection against poisonous vapors.

Even though it was already past midnight, Alexander Caldwell sent word to Mechanicsburg Cemetery to have a grave turned opened. He also ordered a coffin delivered to Ed Shepherd's place. Alexander and his brother went through the woods to their neighbor's home. They instructed Ed's wife, Elizabeth to take the children to safety down the road where they could stay with relatives. At Mechanicsburg the digging began, and by mid-morning the coffin and its shipping box were dropped roadside.

The Caldwell men cared for 30 year old Ed as best they could, but the young husband and father was dead before the day was out. With nothing left to do, the exhausted brothers went home to rest.

Discussion among the roadside crowd was a mix of fear and hysteria. The final consensus was that the departed needed to be buried as soon as possible. Putting as much dense earth between the diseased corpses and other residents in the vicinity would be their best bet.

Several men began digging a double wide grave next to the road. But who would fetch the bodies from out of the home? The terror of coming in direct contact with two bodies dead from the most dread disease of the time was nothing anyone wanted to risk. Finally, William Hopkins stepped forward and agreed to bring them out of the house to the grave by the road. Using the coffin and the wooden crate it was delivered in, Hopkins removed the bodies from the house in two trips. By then, the other men had dug a big enough hole to accommodate the containers. Without help, Hopkins slid the coffin and crate down into the grave as the growing crowd kept their distance. He back-filled the grave with a heaping mound of Boone County topsoil and clay.

Afterwards the cause of death was claimed by officials to be a food born illness; ptomaine poisoning. This was for the public's own peace of mind. A report of cholera was cause for train stations to be passed by and area farm crops to be turned away at grain mills. Churches, merchants, and schools could be abandoned by a cholera scare. Whenever possible, cases of so-called *Black Cholera* went publicly unreported and rumors were quashed as quickly as possible. Some towns even took the extreme measure of changing names to sidestep the stigma placed on them by an outbreak.

At Jamestown's neighbor to the south, that's exactly what happened. Founded and settled as New Elizabeth Town, an Asiatic Cholera outbreak in 1873 made national headlines. Physicians came from as far away as Louisville to help while more of the townspeople fell ill each day. After the disease ran a 25 day course, the small town's reputation was irrevocably in ruins.

At the time of the outbreak, New Elizabeth's population was estimated at 200 persons. Many had been sickened, and 24 died, including one of the treating doctors. In hopes of allaying the stigma, New Elizabeth became known by the shorthand version of its name used on train schedules–Lizton. Many insist those long ago days of late August through mid September in 1873 put a permanent black mark over the growth of a promising place.

The likelihood that both Shepherd son and father died from food poisoning is far-fetched. Dora Caldwell tells of a father coming to visit a son, and when stricken ill, seeks the help of strangers in order to make it to his destination. Edward Shepherd (the surname is spelled on the grave's marker as *Shepard*) was living with his young wife Elizabeth Botts on a newly purchased tract of farmland. Her parents William G Botts and Sarah Moon and her younger siblings are also living on Lost Road. They had all recently moved to Boone County from Ohio.

Ed was born in Pennsylvania and was married to Elizabeth in Ohio. His father was most likely coming from out of state to visit. He probably got off of the stagecoach at the crossing of the Lebanon-Frankfort Road at Mechanicsburg. It makes sense then that he was traveling from the west via foot, thus reaching the Caldwell house before his son's. Following the Strawtown Pike, Mr Shepherd saw the Caldwell home just north of the main road and sought help.

Cholera comes upon a victim by oral contact with expelled fecal matter. This can be from a contaminated water source, or from unwashed hands touching food after an outhouse visit or tending a patient. The effect is alarmingly fast and was often fatal before modern drug therapies were available. From onset of symptoms, to incidence of death can be a matter of hours. On the upside, the pathogen carries a pretty brief life once outside of a live host body. Also, even before treatment was available, only about 20% of those coming in contact with cholera became seriously ill. Some people can have the sickness but show no symptoms as their body rids itself of the offending bacteria.

As for the date dispute, there is evidence beyond Dora's written account recited as a speech to the historical society. He makes some very important points for the argument about the numbers on the grave marker. I feel like Mr Caldwell's date of 1851, not the commonly believed 1864 date, "holds water."

1. Ora Caldwell stated in his remembrance, the event happened in 1851.
2. Even though he would have been a small child in that year (about age 7), and an old man while telling it in 1923 (78), he names the two sisters who were sent to aid the Shepherds–Maranda, and Armilda.
3. Armilda died in 1853.
4. Ed Shepherd and his wife, Elizabeth were married around 1840. They had six living children. The first was born in 1841 and the last in 1848.
5. Although one Botts brother (from Elizabeth Shepherd's family) is still on Lost Road in the 1860 US Census, the Botts parents have moved back to Ohio. The Shepherds are at neither place.
6. Elizabeth never remarried. As late as 1880, about 30 years after this event, she is living in Champagne Illinois with her second youngest son Isaac (Jess) Shepherd.
7. When Elizabeth's father died in 1873, he left her and the children (no mention of Ed) a sum of cash in his will.

Adding to what may have been a whirl of confusion and mistakes, in his transcribed speech, Mr Caldwell hints that the placement of the current marker happened about 50-60 years *after* the two men died.

This may have caused a transcribing error on the dates due to the flourish of records made with old handwriting. The numeral one in is often seen written with a long top tail after the style of European script. Even in the states today, the standard European handwritten numeral one is often mistaken as a four. Also, the worn font of the face is easy to misread. Upon close inspection, what appears to be a "6" is actually a five.

For good measure, I consulted the owners of A&K Monuments in Lebanon. After showing them photos of the Shepard marker it was agreed that the best way to solve this was to find a verifiable stone carved around the same time, from the same area to see if the "date" theory jived. So, off I went to Mechanicsburg Cemetery to have a look. I found a good comparative example at the same cemetery where the grave was originally prepared for Ed Shepherd's father. The Jeremiah Fall stone was carved around the same time as the delayed Shepherd's stone was placed. Judging by the letter styling, this one was carved by the same person who made the *Shepard* stone.

There were no laser-perfect emblazoned type faces available in those days. All stonework was done by hand. Each craftsman had his own lettering repertoire, and in turn, taught those same styles to anyone who apprenticed with him.

Pay close attention to what appears to be a six on the Shepard stone. The number does not have a closed loop on the bottom–it is open, like a five. In the second photo, the lettering and numbers are carved in the same style, including the numeral five, which is clearly different from the six also carved on the face of the Jeremiah Fall headstone.

*

Last of all, there is the legend of The House of the Floating Candle.

This one, I must admit was a real bummer for me. The first time I saw this phenomena I was awestruck and terrified. When I came home that night I couldn't sleep. The next morning when I told my family about the wild adventure I'd been on, my mom rolled her eyes at me and chuckled.

"What could possibly be funny about a demonic house with a candle chasing you?" I demanded.

She asked me a few questions about roads and directions out of town and what the house looked like. And then, quite ceremoniously, she burst my bubble.

"Oh, that's just Ivy Caldwell's house–I'm in Home-Ec with her."

"But mom," I pleaded in disbelief, "That candle was real and there was nobody, as in NO BODY, holding it!"

Laughing again she explained "Well, it's an old house with a single old-fashioned light bulb that just hangs on a wire from the ceiling in the front hall. Every room on the first floor is open to all the others; of course you can see that light from every window! Poor Ivy leaves it on every night because there are always strange cars driving by after dark with no headlights."

Ivy Caldwell was Dora's daughter, and the last surviving Caldwell child of her generation. She never married but was active in county Home-Ec clubs for years, even serving a term as the 1940 County President. The beautiful brick home was built in 1880 when the family moved up the road from their simple wood framed house on the same road closer to Strawtown Pike (where Dora lived when the Shepherd incident happened). Miss Caldwell was said to have possessed a wicked sense of humor, was one heck of a cook and sharp as a tack up to the time of her death in 1982 at 100 years of age.

So, now we're square, Mom and me. She blew the whole titillating terror of the House of the Floating Candle for me, and I discovered that the Shepherds weren't a heartless pioneer family who chucked two men out of their Conestoga wagon to head on down the road to California.

Are You Related to Boone Royalty?

"Honey-Blonde Local Lady is First Queen" (Headline from The Lebanon Reporter, July 1959)

In 1959 a new element was added to the county's annual 4th of July Parade and Celebration. Originally, the pageant was called "Mrs Liberty" in honor of the sponsoring festival. However, that title didn't seem fitting and was only used for one year. Residents much preferred the idea of a "Mrs Boone County." The title representing married women of the county seemed a fitting counterpart to "Miss Boone County" who was first crowned at the 4H Fair in the same year.

Either way, the new pageant may have been a surprising success to the committee. Whether the parade organizers were unprepared, or underfunded to award anything more than a title isn't clear. What is clear, is that Ann Graham, winner of the Mrs Liberty pageant wore a humble cardboard crown at all of her appearances and along the parade route. Her daughter-in-law told me the vivacious and elegant Mrs Graham kept the royal head-wear among her treasured possessions for the rest of her life.

The tradition of Mrs Boone County has continued with an uninterrupted succession of Queens. Boone County hasn't been without an official Mrs Boone since the pageant began. Even though no contest was held in 2009, the 2008 winner, Dawn McNair, graciously stepped in to "serve another term." This little hiccup in the timeline will cause the name of the 2016 winner to be number 57 in the chain of County Lovelies over the past 58 years.

Following is a list of women who have worn the crown. If you don't know a Queen, chances are good that someone near you was Mrs Congeniality, a runner-up or a contender to the court.

1959
The tradition begins with *Ann Graham* as Mrs Liberty

1960s
In 1960, *Laurie Banton* became the first honored with the updated title
Mrs Boone County...and a real crown to boot!

1961 Ann Garaffolo-Goar
1962 Helen Harmon
1963 Karlyn Demaree Cowan
1964 Judy Ritter
1965 Marcia Mossman
1966 Margaret Elliott
1967 Ruth Isenhour
1968 Suzan Burnell
1969 Sandy Obremsky

the 1970s
1970 Karen Boone
1971 Linda Turley
1972 Jane Johnson
1973 Diana Lamb
1974 Carol Snyder
1975 Kay Newman
1976 Kathy Flannery was honored during the National Bicentennial
1977 Carole Toole

1978 LaDonna Skow
1979 Rosie Holloman
the 1980s
1980 Sue Quick
1981 Peggy Eaton
1982 Landa Matthews
1983 Jane Hammock
1984 Sara Lee
1985 Kathleen Leuck
1986 Bonnie Spear LeClave
1987 Corrine Arthur
1988 Kathy Willing
1989 Karen Padgett
the 1990s
1990 Joan Guthridge
1991 Beverly Sloan
1992 Marcia Overfield
1993 Lisa Pierce
1994 Cheryl Brauchla
1995 Beth Demaree
1996 Lana Kruse
1997 Linda Johnson
1998 Linda Jones
1999 Margie Thomas
the new century 2000
2000 Lynn Shaw
2001 Lori French
2002 Cindy Hume
2003 Rachel Frazier
2004 Jama Gillihan
2005 Ginger Truitt
2006 Kathy Lukes
2007 Karla Peebles
2008 & 2009 Dawn McNair

(although the pageant was on hiatus in 2009, the role was still
filled by the previous year's winner)
2010 Vicki Dusek
2011 Terri Batts
2012 Jennifer Sherrill
2013 Angela Hensell
2014 Anita Bowen
2015 Mikki Folden
2016 Kim Morgan

In 2014 responsibility for the Mrs Boone County pageant
shifted directorship. Created originally and overseen as a
committee under the umbrella of the 4th of July festivities, the
scepter was passed. Since that change in 2014, past Mrs Boone
County winners have planned and promoted the event. With the
slow disappearance of locally owned banks (formerly the largest
underwriters as a group) pageant funding changes were made as
well.

Those participating must be sponsored by a local not-for-
profit group performing civic or charitable service within the
community. The court of ladies is judged using much of the
original 1959 criteria for choosing the County's best
representative.

In announcing Ann Graham as the original Queen, a *Lebanon
Reporter* article noted some of the rigorous standards for judging.
Each woman had been scrutinized on their personal contribution
to the community at large, personality, decorum and poise.

Contestants today are encouraged to seek community
sponsorship and donations to help cover pageant expenses.
Looking into the future, the group of past winners plans to bring
back many old traditions of the Queenly Reign. Clearly, the
future of this well-loved part of the 4th of July fun is in able
hands.

Reign of the Extension Homemakers

$\sim\!\infty\!\sim$

"Husky Children, Healthy Husbands, and Happy Homemakers" (BCEH motto adopted 1937)

The Indiana Extension Homemaker's Association was first organized in 1913. In 1936 it took root in Boone County when township clubs were formed. The women adopted their motto and creed for Boone County Extension Homemakers at their first conference in 1937. Lead by a Miss Beadle of Purdue University, the all-day meeting set forth the focus of projects and studies for the coming year. The subjects of concentration were decided as: Posture, Menu Planning, Protective and Corrective Foods, and Refreshments for Special Occasions.

Endearingly called "Home-Ec Clubs" The BCEH was not the first women's group organized in the county. All sorts of sororities, public health, domestic sciences, political concerns, charitable aid, creative expression, poetry appreciation, high culture, book clubs, library and hospital guilds, card clubs, church boosters–and as many other reasons for a gathering as one could think of–were in existence long before Home-Ec came along. All forms of club membership and association were an important part of life for both men and women from the earliest years of settlement.

The new program rolled out in the 1930s certainly stood out as a lifeline to rural women in all corners of the county. The small groups provided a social outlet, education, networking and sharing among many who might be living an otherwise solitary existence.

Always supporters of 4H, the clubs started the popular Open Show days at the annual 4H fair. Women can participate in a variety of categories, win prizes, and even go on to compete at the state level. A popular fund raising event for the Homemakers is the baked goods auction at the end of Open Show. There's always been a lot of love, pride and raw competitiveness baked into every entry. The auction creates some good-natured bidding wars and ego boosts for those whose entries glean top dollar.

The many volunteers, participants, vendors and visitors at the Boone County 4H fair have always counted on the Home-Ec ladies to feed them a wholesome meal over the course of the fair. Until recent years, food service was centered at a semi-outdoor kitchen area known as "the Bee Hive." Here, big plates of tasty foods were served up with the centerpiece always being the pie slices. Home-Ec members knew how to bake! The assortment was mind boggling, and every piece was a blue-ribbon-worthy bite of heaven. Inside, the old Hive was always hotter than Hades, but the club volunteers served it all up with grace and a smile.

Fund raising is done to offset the tiny dues charged to members. Even in 2012, the annual fee for membership was set at $7 per year. Still, the thrifty women have always found ways to underwrite ribbons along with cash prizes for Open Show entries. They also host workshops and programs (like massive elementary school book giveaways) while managing to make large cash donations for worthy community causes.

When the kitchen at the community building of the new 4H grounds needed equipment, the Homemakers stepped up. The group as a whole was instrumental in getting the original facility funded and built by the county in 1959.

Home-Ec clubs aren't all work and fundraising. The women also take cultural trips, host a Quilt Show and Bee, hold an annual Christmas Luncheon and are represented on the County Fair Board.

Enthusiastic supporters of the 1976 Bicentennial celebration, the Homemakers were integral to coordinating the completion of the Bicentennial Sampler. The only thing larger than the 10'x12' quilted "sampler" was the participation county-wide. Each township's Home-Ec club solicited patch contributions showcasing needle artistry representative of their township. This was done in cooperation with area coordinators. The result, now on display in the courthouse rotunda, was the end product of more than 1000 hands-on contributors.

The front of the sampler is a county map with each township outlined. Within each township, several stitched and patched pieces depict important aspects of the local community. Upon close inspection of Perry Township, an embroidered gavel can be found–symbolizing my own Mom's service as the bicentennial year County President of BCEH. The edge and backside of the piece consist of small patches made by individuals. Each name represents a committee member, a service organization, a local official or office, or a longtime landmark business.

The original intent was for the sampler to be hung from the courthouse rotunda for the yearlong celebration. After the year was up, the Bicentennial Committee planned to have the quilt laminated to protect it from fading or deterioration. Unbeknownst to those who chose the rotunda as the ultimate display spot, the fabric and stitching was protected naturally by the filtering effect of the courthouse's double layered dome of stained glass protected by an exterior shell. Forty years after the

United States celebrated its 200th birthday, the decoration that was only supposed to be on display for one year is still in place.

People visiting the courthouse, whether for business or pleasure, are often seen hugging the second story marble railing to photograph the beloved sampler.

The club creed written up in 1937 read~

We believe in the present and its opportunities, in the future and its promise; in everything that makes life large and lovely, in the divine joy of living and helping others; and so we endeavor to pass on to others that which has benefited us, reaching the pinnacle of economic perfection, in the improving, enlarging, and endearing the greatest institution in the world,...THE HOME.

A listing of the Past County Presidents is provided in this book. The women are named with the year they began serving their term as head of all the Boone County Extension Homemakers. The number who served as president of their own township's club, worked on a committee or held membership would fill an entire book many times the size of this. Membership was incredibly widespread, even becoming very popular among the non-rural population.

If there is a favorite food traditional to your Boone County gatherings at table, chances are pretty good it was once a recipe shared at a Home-Ec meeting—Husky, Healthy, Happy!

All citizens of The State of Boone have benefited greatly from the quiet work of the Extension Homemakers

Past County Presidents Listing

note: The womens' first names are noted where available. Early on, most were listed only by their husband's name.

1930s

1937 Mrs Paul Lane–1938 Mrs Lester Flanigan
1939 Mrs Hassil Schenck

1940s

1940 Miss Ivy Caldwell–1941 Mrs AV Van Huss
1942 Mrs CC Madion–1943 Mrs Glen Groves
1944 Mrs George Daggy–1945 Mrs Thelma (Earl) Dye
1946 Mrs Duane Thompson–1947 Mrs Laura (Wendell)
Morton
1948 Mrs Leland Burchell–1949 Mrs Carl Witt

1950s

1950 Mrs Guy Stewart–1951 Mrs JR Stewart
1952 Mrs Anthony Kincaid–1953 Mrs Verna Mullikin
1954 Mrs Hassil Schenck–1955 Mrs TW Saltmarsh

1956 Mrs Lloyd Miller–1957 Mrs Viola (Earl) Roberts
1958 Mrs Hazel (William) Delong–1959 Mrs Alyce (Karl) Miller

1960s
1960 Mrs Leah May (Elton) Williams–1961 Mrs Edith (Dale)
Martin
1962 Mrs Martha (Wilber) Whitehead–1963 Mrs Doris
(Brewer) Demaree
1964 Mrs Shirley (Jon) Woody–1965 Mrs Anna (Frank) Poynter
1966 Mrs Lucille (FL) McDonald–1967 Mrs Donna Swank (Ed)
Rice
1968 Mrs Ruth (Robert) Pickering–1969 Mrs Shirley (Max)
Lowery

1970s
1970 Mrs Lima (Golda) Ragsdale–1971 Mrs John Luff
1972 Mrs Leota (John) Shinn–1973 Mrs Helen (Fred)
Andrew1974 Mrs Jane (Rudy) Gibbs
1975 Mrs Carolyn (Frank) Miller–bicentennial term
1976 Mrs Hope (Larry) Pittman–1977 Mrs Lynn (Don) Kenyan
1978 Mrs Mildred (Nathan) Collins–1979 Mrs Joan (Leo)
Busenbarrick

1980s
1980 Mrs Joan (Leo) Busenbarrich served a back-to-back term.
This was the first in a trend of several multi-year terms to follow.
    A few single-year terms were interspersed, but most began
the habit of serving two years.
1981 Mrs Pat Smith
1982/1983 Mrs Ruth (Otis) Burrus
1984/1985 Mrs Joan (Robert) Hysong
1986/1987 Mrs Diana (Robert) Lamb
1988 Mrs Charlene (Byron) Hackett
1989 Mrs Judy (Herb) Bollinger

1990s

1990 (as well as the previous 1989) Mrs Judy (Herb) Bollinger
1991/1992 Mrs Judi (Lynn) Wilson
1993/1994 Mrs Bev (Sam) Ramsey
1995/1996 Mrs Debbie (Sam) Kremer
1997/1998 Mrs Patty (Mark) Nichols
1999 Mrs Beverly (Gary) Moore

2000s

2000 Mrs Beverly (Gary) Moore
2001/2002 Mrs Virginia (Paul) Hart
2003/2004 Mrs Bonnie (Dale) Smith
2005 Mrs Clairbelle (Joe) Robinson–2006 Mrs Anita (Mike)
Sedwick
2007/2008 Mrs Shirley (Marvin) Lasley
2009/2010 Mrs Patty (Mark) Nichols
2011/2012 Mrs Kimberly (Bill) Westfall
2013/2014 Mrs Bridgette (Walter) Burtner

Man, Beast or Apparition?

❦

"An' the Gobble-uns 'll git you, ef you don't watch out!" (from James Whitcomb Riley's beloved poem Little Orphant Annie)

A little something to raise your neck hair is always available in the State of Boone. Ghost hunters are in love with our county for its haunted barns–where despondent farmers hanged themselves or blew out their brains after a dismal crop yield.

A janitor's ghost menaced the stairway-to-nowhere in Lebanon's old high school; terrifying students by the score. Meanwhile, a female apparition ocassionally roams the halls of the old Witham Hospital building.

Driving along Holiday road to visit the deadly haunted "Hundred Foot" bridge can only happen if you don't chicken-out when moans and whispers crawl out of the woods and into your car while passing the hidden graves at Cox's-Old Eagle Cemetery.

Moonlit sightings of the Gray Man along the road to Elizaville are common too–when you're alone, and it's late.

Every concrete railroad bridge in Boone County holds the same regrettable history. You know–"the Irish worker who fell headfirst into the slurry and was buried alive because the foreman refused to stop work to pull him out." Teenagers from every generation are sure they've heard pitiful moans emitting from underneath the tracks.

Each Boone township has a Lover's Lane, and every one of these parking hot-spots claims rights to being the authentic site of the most famous of all the spook-tales ever told– presented here in its most stripped down form:

...amorous teens hear scratching noises on the roof of the car–brave boy gets out to investigate–impatient girl gets fed up with waiting and exits the car–girl finds boyfriend hanging from a meat hook...

A pair of young men conjured up the spoof of two ghosts at Mechanicsburg Cemetery in 1864. They did it to keep an old moocher from grazing his horse during a long summer drought. Their plan worked. The offending squatter was frightened away. He never turned his nag out on the graveyard again. Their convincing "scare" also triggered years of retelling as the legendary "Twin Ghosts of Mechanicburg" chiller.

The Mozingo ghost story reported in 1886 might actually have been based in truth; at least in a probable-cause kind of way. Not a trace remains of the live-in housekeeper employed by the Mozingos. Folks scratched their head when the family of meager means brought her with them from Kentucky. After their young house-girl vanished, the rather shifty branch of the Mozingo clan packed up and skipped town in the middle of the night.

The house Mozingos rented was owned by area farmer DA Caldwell. Even though neighbors were a bit suspicious of the dirt-poor tinker's family with a servant, everyone sort of minded their own business. In fact, folks on the street were secretly relieved when the distasteful family vacated. Being close to all Lebanon had to offer, Caldwell had eager new renters for the home no time.

That's when everyone took notice there might be something amiss. The Wyatt Mires family was thrilled to move into the convenient address. However within days, their oldest son refused to sleep alone in his bedroom. The boy complained that he was being terrorized nightly by a headless specter. He insisted a female ghost woke him each night between midnight and one while stroking her icy hand over his brow.

The odd happenings at the rental ran as an item in newspapers. Except for the mysterious young "housekeeper," everyone else in the news article was verifiable as real–most of them are buried now at Oak Hill. Several folks hypothesized the young girl was actually a stolen child the family used as a slave and then murdered. Unfortunately, the Mozingo ghost tale is a hard one to chase down. The house which stood two lots to the south of the tracks on Meridian Street was razed long ago.

Hearing these stories about the boy's nightly trauma, the town Marshal investigated the rumors of the Mozingo house-girl's plight. The Marshal was surprised to hear from neighbors that many had asked Mrs Mozingo about the girl's whereabouts recently. Curiosity stirred when several days passed without anyone seeing her hanging laundry in the yard and going about her other chores. The wife told the neighbors the ungrateful girl had "run-off." Even with suspicions of the neighbors to go on, no evidence of foul play was discovered. As an extra measure, deputies were instructed to spend several days "fishing" for remains in wells around town before the matter was put to rest.

The Mires' family moved out. No one knows if DA Caldwell's rental was ever occupied by paying tenants again .

Out in the country, kids have been sure they were sleeping over some angry Indian tribe burial ground for generations. The perpetual fear is fueled by recycled stories of wailing babies petrified in trees, Indian maidens fully engulfed inside of an ancient oak named "Old Pisa," and the ever-present threat of howling wolf spirits or scalped missionaries. It's a wonder anyone under the age of 30 has ever gotten a wink of sleep since time began in Boone County.

An extensive telling of an incident near Big Springs in 1883 ran in *The Zionsville Times* and a few other local papers. This one was especially chilling since the three men involved were stalwart pillars of piety and reputed non-drunkards. If they weren't making it up–someone must have picked the wrong mushrooms to serve in their dinner stew.

The reliable men gave an account of a night that started as a coon hunt and ended with their entire party shaken and wide-eyed with terror. They fully believed they must have stumbled upon an unholy city of witches, ghosts and demons. Entering the woods near Slabtown the men said they were confronted by a fire-eyed skeleton wielding a 20 foot saber.

When the experienced hunters fired their guns in unison at the threatening bones, the once-single skeleton shattered into a thousand tiny ones. Each had a different head–the next one more gruesome than the last. Some had human faces in a state of obvious decomposition; others looked like horses or lizards. The demonic creatures skittered off into the woods, shaking the ground as they went; shrieking and wailing their unearthly screams.

Let's go out on a limb here and assume that Slabtown raccoons were safe from hunters for many years afterwards.

The Thorntown Gorilla

There ought to be a fine or penalty for anybody spreading an untrue tale which may create a wave of terrorism in the community" (William Davies on Gorilla sightings–Tipton Indiana)

More than all of the other whoppers, legends, tales and woofin in Boone County, one reigns supreme. The whole thing was a hoax, but it is just so ingrained in the lore of our land, its too good to be swallowed up by time. And so it continues to this day–in many ways. An occasional good-natured note might appear on local police blotters, or a Facebook post or a Tweet. Sometimes a newspaper clipping surfaces of a man in a dentist's chair getting a check-up and dishing on the old days. Even the Thorntown library occasionally hosts a celebration in honor of the vicious terror!

If you're a lucky sort, someone told you the story while camping in your own backyard, on a moonless night, with nothing defending you from the wrath of the wilderness but the flap of a patched-up army tent.

Residents of Thorntown know the best prank ever began in 1949; the summer the Gorilla first emerged.

The warm months of 1949 were a nervous time across the heartland. Sons and brothers called to service against the evils of Hitler's plan to rule the world were trying hard to forget the past and resettle into "normalcy." Then a new era known as the Cold War began, piling on another layer worries. All of this was brewing while ration books, air raid drills, and too many other sacrifices great and small were painfully fresh recollections. To top it all off, the whole world was fighting yet another evil–polio.

No matter how hot the summer days, no matter how much the Old Swimming Hole's cooling waters beckoned, every kid was strictly ordered to stay out. A half million people were dying every year from polio world-wide. Those who survived the sickness were left crippled or suffered other lifelong health problems. The largest outbreaks happened in swimming season during hot weather. Understandably, folk's nerves were frayed to the edge.

In Thorntown, a certain young fellow by the name of Gobby Jones didn't do much to lift the spirits of others. In fact, outside of working, he did little besides fish and brag extensively about his triumphant catches. Even on the day he was scheduled to be saved by the waters of Baptism for his exaggerations and loafing, Gobby chose to skip out and keep his pole in the water downstream.

Gobby kept angling as the preacher and a whole congregation stood waiting for him and his wayward soul on the creek bank. When asked later why he never showed up to be cleansed and reborn, Gobby responded in a matter-of-fact way that he wanted to stick around and catch all the fish who'd swum through the blessed waters.

A few young men in Gobby's circle had about all they could stand of him with his big fish tales and lazing-about attitude. His coworkers Asher Cones, Homer Birge and George Coffman started plotting. Why they were so agitated by the guy isn't really clear. Per human nature it seems there's always somebody, in every group of people, who has a knack for monopolizing conversations and making everyone's eyes role. Gobby must have been *that guy* in Thorntown leading up to the summer of 1949.

So the story goes that these three fellows got together and cooked up a scheme to scare the b-jeebers out of Gobby. They hoped to startle him so profoundly that Jones would never have the nerve to pick up a fishing pole again. Once freed from his constant boasting, they, and all the folks around town, could finally have some peace.

The trio decided that scaring Gobby off the banks of Sugar Creek would best be accomplished by the threat of a wild animal attack. As a group they had some excellent skill sets at hand. Homer was a welder by trade. His wife Pearl could sew anything. Asher was a real thinker– a good logistics man, and George was strong, fast and possessed a love of pranks and adventure.

They agreed their best bet was to build a bear suit. Surely coming face-to-face with a raging bear would cure Gobby of his nonstop fishing and the whoppers he told, once and for all.

Birge remembered his dad had an old horsehair coat tucked away in a closet that he hadn't worn in years. Pearl noted that one coat wouldn't yield enough hide for the big plans Homer and his friends had cooking. Cones suddenly recalled another old guy in town, Mr Bill Strong, had a horsehair coat too. Bill Strong had owned and worn the shaggy thing every winter for as long as anyone could remember.

On a sultry summer afternoon Asher Cones sauntered up to the Strong's door and asked Mrs Strong if she wouldn't mind selling him that coat? Mrs Strong, elated at the thought that her husband could be fitted with something a little more modern, struck a deal with Asher and the coat was sold for cash that day. Giddy to receive the kingly sum of ten dollars for a ratty old coat, Mrs Strong never asked a single question.

As a side note, a couple of years down the road, Frank Birge (Homer's brother) married Bill Strong's daughter– and that's how Boone County came to have its treasured ex-pat Dick Birge.

Part number one of their grand plan was in motion. The group turned Pearl loose with her masterful seamstress skills. She took the coats apart and began the work of sewing them onto an old pair of coveralls as a base. Homer worked to form a lightweight wire frame for the creature's head, welding all pieces delicately in place.

The trio's bear suit was coming together. Old Gobby would be scared wordless in no time!

They added a fiery red felt tongue and cut jagged teeth from tin. They coated the teeth with white paint to make them stand out. The best bit of engineering was saved for the eyes of the bear. A pair of cat's eye marbles were mounted at the eye holes to reflect light with an eerie golden-green glow. Small slits were left under the marbles to allow the wearer to see. As a final touch, small battery operated lights were rigged to contact points on a clothes pin. When the wearer bit down on the spring loaded pin, the eyes lit up. Together, they had successfully created the scariest demon-bear imaginable.

Cones, Birge and Coffman all admitted later, the bear suit would have never passed for more than it was upon close examination; a couple of old coats sewn onto coveralls with a head that had to be held in place by hand at all times. They also said the widespread panic and publicity they stirred up was way more than they'd ever bargained for.

Once their masterpiece was ready, they decided to try it out on Gobby in broad daylight. They reasoned that if it would pass muster at a bit of a distance during the day, it would be extra terrifying at night. Homer put on the suit and waited as George led Gobby to the spot where the terrifying bear lay hiding in wait. As the pair walked along the creek bank, the brush on the opposite shore began violently rustling. Suddenly, a large dark figure appeared.

Gobby spied the giant critter and was seized with panic. He bolted up a steep embankment to the flat land above and ran like he was being chased by the devil. He felt his wallet bounce out of his pocket but didn't bother to stop. Gobby didn't quit running until he got back into town. Once there, he breathlessly told everyone who would listen about the wild gorilla running loose along Sugar Creek.

Gorilla?

None of the creators of the beast could let it be known that their monster was meant to be a bear without blowing their cover–so–if Gobby saw a gorilla, then it sure wasn't a bear!

That evening, Asher and Homer decided to try it out in the dark. They headed to a lonely patch of road. Homer got out at a curve near a place called Baker's Pit. He ran into the cornfield and waited for Asher's headlights to return. Even though the whole test was planned, Asher Cones said in a "confession" he wrote late in his life, that seeing that thing walk out in front of him made the hair raise straight up on the back of his neck.

The fellas knew they had a winner! Once his experience was solidly confirmed by others, old Gobby's fish tales would be a thing of the past.

Those who said they didn't believe were put in line as the next victims. The three worked out a system for identifying cars carrying doubters as they drove out into the corn-lined country roads. Together, they developed schemes for making both a convincing appearance and stealthy escape.

On one occasion, Homer and George brought some nonbelievers out to Baker's Pit for some "night fishing." Asher waited in the suit near the edge of the water. As the boat approached his position, Cones began shaking limbs on some shrubby brush. The fishermen started making a fuss about hearing odd noises while shining their flashlights up along the marshy bank. When the gorilla with his eerie flashing eyes and terrifying teeth looked at them full-on one of the intended victims, Amos Copas, had to be forcibly held back from jumping into the water. Copas almost scared the conspirators to death–Asher, George and Homer all knew the poor guy couldn't swim a single stroke!

For weeks that summer the three took turns wearing the suit and accosting carloads of drivers; especially groups of girls. During the gorilla's reign of terror, newspapers from both coasts and all the way from north to south carried the stories coming out of Thorntown. The hysteria took root in the minds of other Hoosiers too. Soon sheriffs as far away as Lawrence County were busy patrolling for gorillas.

Circus and carnival shows were questioned, zoos were asked to take inventories–but no reports of missing gorillas turned up. Law enforcement and the whole community was puzzled. How could the summer cornfields suddenly be teeming with jungle primates?

A buzz started when someone cooked up the idea of "gorilla drives" to be carried out on-foot and by air. On July 17th, a posse of 40 farmers armed with shotguns and rifles spent an entire day combing area fields attempting to track down the beast. Pilots were recruited to aid the searchers from above.

Asher, George and Homer got scared. People were going crazy and "seeing" gorillas in places the three had never even been before. Folks were also getting angry. One man reported that he'd lost a full week of wages because his wife was too afraid to let him leave the house.

Once the guns came out and air support was called in, the boys decided it was time to call an end to their fun. They had achieved their original goal weeks before; that first encounter had been enough to cure Gobby from his non-stop fishing and bragging.

In Asher Cones' tell-all letter he revealed that years later, Homer, upon hearing that Gobby lay dying at the hospital, went to visit him. Homer told Gobby the whole story. Gobby listened, but refused to believe a word of what Homer said. He looked his friend straight in the eyes and told him, "I know what I saw, and I saw a gorilla. It wasn't someone dressed up!"

Oddly enough, the case was "solved" one day after the boys quit. Once again, newspapers across the nation jumped to report follow up stories on the Thorntown Gorilla Terror.

On July 18th, after local farmers and pilots had spent hours the previous day storming corn fields, Thorntown Marshals Sam Allen and Ralph Davidson cracked the case. They apprehended a deranged woman in the brush along Sugar Creek. She was wearing a dark colored dress, crouching amid the weeds and

1

babbling. Her brown hair was matted with dirt and leaves. They estimated her age to be around 40. She refused or was unable to give her name. She kept questioning the Marshals asking them multiple times

"Do you think I've scared them long enough?"

Authorities immediately initiated proceedings for her commitment.

After the woman was taken into custody, the gorilla sightings mostly stopped...in Boone County. It seems that hysterical agitation is quite contagious. By August, a gorilla was spotted on multiple occasions 40 or 50 miles away in Tipton County. In late September, all of Columbia City was trembling in fear of the gorilla. Even though witnesses said the animal they spotted looked more like a panther–authorities refused to rule out a possible gorilla infestation.

In 2007, two men from Boone County reported an early morning encounter with a hominoid creature as they drove home from shift work in Indianapolis. Around 5:30am on highway 421 between Waugh and Rosston the two were in separate vehicles. The driver in the lead car spotted a large animal in his path and swerved, but his co-worker didn't have time to react. The second man clipped the creature with the fender of his Ford Explorer knocking it to the ground. The man-animal tried several times to stand while howling with agony. Finally it scurried away on all fours and disappeared into the treeline. The incident is recorded on the web site www.BigfootEncounters.com

Suppose someone found a dusty old bear suit in an attic?

———————

~*~

This retelling is dedicated to the memory of
Asher Cones 1913-2014
George Coffman 1908-1993
Homer Birge 1910-1994
...and Gobby of course, who is probably lounging in heaven at the greatest fishing hole ever!...

~*~

~*~

Many thanks to Dick Birge and Phyllis Meyers for sharing the great bones of this story! I'm sure that if these three friends were still living, they would be shocked to know how widespread the effect of their prank was that summer. If nothing else, the gorilla gave folks something besides their troubles to worry about—something that they could defend themselves against.

Time Capsules
Made and Found
and Made Again

When the cornerstone was laid at Lebanon in 1909 for the new county courthouse, an assortment of items was added into a niche specially carved for that purpose.

The contents were selected as a representation of life in Boone County at the time the fourth seat of government was erected. A listing of the saved items was published in the *The Lebanon Pioneer*. The cornerstone time capsule, still in place, contains the following items–

- Holy Bible
- An exhaustive list of names pertinent to the times–the list includes both William H Taft and James Sherman (newly elected first term President and Vice President of the United States), the US Senators from Indiana and the 9th District Representative, State Officers, Elected and Appointed County Officers, members of the Boone County Bar Association and of the Building Committee for the new Court House.
- Current copies of local newspapers– *The Lebanon Patriot, The Lebanon Reporter, The Pioneer, The Thorntown Argus-Enterprise, The Whitestown Dispatch, Advance Friday Caller, Jamestown Press*

- A High School Pennant (unspecified school)
- Various News Clippings
- The lock from the Court House built in 1857
- A compilation of Historic Data
- Photos of the County Council, County Commissioners and Advisory Committee members
- Souvenir Spoon depicting the Old Court House (a very popular item in its day)
- Photo of the *Old* Court House
- Twenty Souvenir postcards of county scenes
- Directory of Boone Schools
- 20th Century corn, oats, wheat, timothy and clover
- Money
- Button and Badge from the GAR (Grand Army of the Republic)
- Souvenir of the "largest regiment furnishing soldiers" from Boone during the War of the Rebellion
- Badge from the Women's Relief Corps
- Full roster of officers and members of the Masonic Order of Boone County
- Roster of Grand Lodge Officers of F&AM (Free & Accepted Masons)
- A Program outlining the Ceremony commemorating dedication day (November 30, 1909)
- Lambskin Apron
- Note by Caldwell and Drake (the Indianapolis-based construction firm who built the courthouse)
- An inventory list of the items contained in the box

Later, another time capsule was left encased fully in copper in the new courthouse. It was assembled in 1916 to honor the centennial of Indiana's Statehood. While Peggy Brogan was working at the courthouse in the 1970s, she stumbled on the centennial time capsule during renovations and always hoped that she would be around to see its opening. After a 30 year career, Brogan retired and handed the care and keeping over to Jamey Hickson at the Ralph W Stark Heritage Department at the Lebanon Public Library.

In January 2016, the hundred year old container was unsealed. Peggy was there beside Jamey and others. Found inside were the Celebration Committee's Meeting Minutes Book, two Guest Registers, some correspondence, photos of Boone County's various state centennial celebrations, a large collection of news clippings and lots of "ephemera."

Currently, the items to be sealed away for finding and reminiscing over in 2116 are being gathered. I am so honored to report that this book, along with my other title, *Boone County*, will be among the surprises awaiting Boone residents 100 years in the future.

I'm sure it's going to take 100 years for the grin to fade from my face!

www.ingramcontent.com/pod-product-compliance
Lightning Source LLC
Chambersburg PA
CBHW071223090426
42736CB00014B/2954